# A CALL TO INSPIRE

## *Bridging the Wide Chasm Between God's Will for Our Lives and Ours*

Ken and Linda Parkany

ISBN 978-1-64458-111-7 (paperback)
ISBN 978-1-64458-112-4 (digital)

Christian Faith Publishing, Inc.
832 Park Avenue
Meadville, PA 16335
www.christianfaithpublishing.com

Printed in the United States of America

There is no greater joy in life than to sense the Holy Spirit
at work, for we are all instruments in His orchestra of
Divine Harmony.

—Ken Parkany

To the glory of God, the memory of parents and loved ones and others who inspired us. To our children, their spouses, and our grandchildren—may you always remember that God brings people into our lives for a moment, a lifetime or a season, but always for a reason to inspire us that we may inspire others.

# Contents

# Acknowledgments

*A Call to Inspire*, as you'll see, is due to the grace of God. We thank you, Lord.

As a 1950s youth passionate about sports, the outdoors, and, in Linda's case, dancing and "tomboyish" activities, writing or authoring a book was never on our radar.

Baseball, gymnastics, fishing, and hunting preoccupied my time and my mind. While Linda was a straight-A student, education seemed like a necessary evil to me. A mysterious traumatic confrontation between me and my second-grade teacher led me to dislike teachers and school. I settled for being an average student.

My secondary school average grades were threatened in my final semester of high school. Miss Andrews granted me immeasurable grace—a letter grade D in English, enabling me to graduate. I made it thus far through pure persistence instilled in me by hardworking blue-collar parents who survived the Great Depression. They expected me to pursue all things to completion. Their generation called it: "stick-to-itiveness."

Apparently, I was educationally an underachiever by choice, for I excelled in baseball and gymnastics. Family and friends were well aware of my successful fishing prowess. I survived high school, yet it is a mystery how I managed to get accepted to college and earn an engineering degree while working full-time evenings and living at home. Even more puzzling was how I later managed to acquire an MBA during evening classes while employed as a frequent-traveling aerospace engineer. Somehow, I managed concurrently to be a responsible husband and father.

Perhaps the bigger mystery is how I acquired a condition in my late twenties called, in Latin, *cacoethes scribendi*, or an uncontrollable desire to write, that led to a freelance writing career with no rejection letters, and a stint as freelance weekly outdoor columnist with one of the largest and oldest newspapers in continuous circulation: Connecticut's Hartford Courant. The latter experience led to memberships in the New England Outdoor Writer's Association and the Outdoor Writer's Association of America.

I acknowledge my achievements in spite of a lackluster educational beginning for a reason. They were not due to any exceptional ability. Total credit for the above mysteries and my persistence over resistance is all due to God's grace and His divine intervention in my life. He put the right people—parents, my wife, family members, friends, and yes, teachers—in the right place at the right time to inspire me.

Randall Harris, compiler of *The Contemporaries Meet the Classics on the Holy Spirit* (Howard 2004), stated: "There is always the temptation to see spiritual gifts for one's own glory. But there is an eternal principle— gifts are always intended to bring the people of God closer to Him." The authors' experiences in *A Call to Inspire* were all divinely orchestrated, therefore God gets the glory. Though Linda and I have used our gifts to receive the fruit of His spirit and have decided to share them with readers, we cannot honestly claim full authorship.

I am indebted to Linda, my wife, best friend—a devoted mother and grandmother. Her care-giving skills and instincts made her perfectly suitable for a career as a registered nurse and a Stephen Minister. She is my best sounding board and constructive critic. Linda suggests that she is indebted to me for encouraging her to write her memoirs, not for publication, but for sharing with our children, their spouses, and the twelve grandchildren who have blessed our lives. Yet, not surprisingly, some of her memoirs found their way into this book.

The authors are grateful to the following for their time and wise theological counsel after reading the manuscript: Dr. Lewis Gregory, President, Source Ministries International, Atlanta, Georgia; Pastor Jeff Harter, Chaplain with Lutheran Senior Services and Minister of Reconciliation for the Lutheran Church Missouri Synod, St. Louis, Missouri; Pastor E. J. Sweeney, BA Trinity, MDiv, Yale; and Charles

Kaucher, MDiv, Gordon-Conwell Theological Seminary. Their insightful comments helped us to better understand and therefore emphasize how God works in mysterious yet ordinary ways.

One individual, Winston O. Abbott (1909–1990) of South Windsor, Connecticut, author and founding publisher of Inspiration House Publishers, was a dear friend and mentor. His five books of poetic prose, *Come Climb My Hill, Come Walk Among the Stars, Have You Heard the Cricket Song, Letters from Chickadee Hill, and Sing with the Wind*, still inspire today. For ten years, Winston shared not only his time and wisdom with me, but numerous lunch hours of camaraderie. I will always be indebted to him, his memory, and his legacy of inspiring thousands, perhaps millions by now, around the globe through his books.

Linda and I want to thank family and friends who gave us the opportunity to share our experiences with many groups in churches over the years. We are eternally grateful for God's guidance, inspiration, and using us as His instruments so that others might have a glimpse of the Holy Spirit's power. As we spiritually mature, Linda and I know from experience that power can burst forth like "rivers of flowing water" as God intended (John 7:37–39, ESV).

To teachers everywhere, who faithfully persist, especially in my case, in spite of underachieving attitudes, I say thank you. Thanks to family and friends for their encouragement, especially Chris DiCio, a retired school teacher who read and re-read the manuscript and provided clarity. Thanks also to the editors and staff of Christian Faith Publishing for their professional assistance.

Lastly, there is a family member, my uncle Steve Parkany, whose passion for fishing inspired me so deeply that I penned a true fishing story about him that was accepted and published in the *Pennsylvania Angler,* later renamed *Pennsylvania Angler & Boater Magazine* in June 1975. That event motivated me to continue honing my "wordsmithing" skills that has now led to *A Call to Inspire*. Thank you, Uncle Steve.

The word inspire was originally used of a divine or supernatural
being, in the sense to 'impart a truth or idea to someone'
—Oxford Dictionary

Rebecca VanOrder age 15

Supernaturally inspired – the authors' granddaughter
was unaware she had drawn an impressionistic image
of a person's head until the Holy Spirit revealed it
to the author many weeks later. Do you see it?

# Introduction

Why does there seem to be such a great chasm between God's will for our lives and our burning desire to see His will happen in us? For many Christians, that question seems to be a life-long quest. So when and how does God's will for our lives happen? Does it happen suddenly or gradually? Does it just show up in our lap, so to speak, or must we strive for it? And finally, what is God's role and ours?

The above questions may have you thinking: *What are the authors talking about? What is God's will?* That's okay. It's an indication that God is likely already touching your heart. And no matter where you are on your walk with God, the experiences you are about to read may reveal more to you than you might expect.

If we believe what the Bible says, then what is it like to experience God's will? His will is unique to each one of us, but the Apostle Paul says in his letter to the Romans that it is a process that requires action on our part (Rom. 12:1–2). *A Call to Inspire* is how the authors surrendered to God's Holy Spirit in prayer, thereby allowing Him to use us in an amazing series of divine appointments, interventions, and even brief reminders to serve His purpose. We believe *A Call to Inspire* can ignite God's Holy Spirit—His Holy Flame—in you. Doing so can allow you to live your life's story in a way that God intended and in ways you cannot even imagine.

Today, if we are seeking information or answers to certain questions, our natural go-to is to ask Siri or search the internet. But let me suggest another more reliable and accurate source, one that's been around for more than two thousand years. With the Bible as our guide, let me assure you that source is spiritual in nature and both supernatural and mysterious in action. All born again believers possess that source—the third person of the Trinity, God's Holy Spirit.

Without realizing it, Christians seem to be bent on doing God's work their way. But what if we would let God use us to do His work His way? In doing so, we have the opportunity to witness His intentions for our lives, for that is what pleases God and gives Him glory. Our ways are natural, His are supernatural. The Bible is filled with such examples of God using ordinary people supernaturally—Moses, David, Joseph, Joshua, Gideon and yes, even enemies of God's people. And Luke's account of the disciples after Jesus's death and resurrection in the book of Acts is only a small sampling of how the Holy Spirit used the disciples after Pentecost to spread the Gospel.

After listening to us share our stories, one pastor stated during his sermon, "Here was a clear example of how God used two ordinary people to do extraordinary things." Is God still using ordinary people today to enact His will upon us and others who trust Him to do so? Is His Holy Spirit still active? If you have any doubts, we suggest you delay your final decision until after reading *A Call to Inspire*—a personal and intimate guide to the Holy Spirit. You will see how the authors let the Holy Spirit use them in answer to a simple prayer, followed by trust and obedience. Linda and I have been humbled and blessed beyond our expectation and imagination. Linda and I praise God for heaping so many blessings upon us; we glorify God by sharing our divine appointments, interventions, and brief reminders; and we stand in awe of His presence in our midst, so much so that we call our journeys an "Awedyssee." It's a play on the word for wandering journey—odyssey. God's role is the supernatural "awe" and "see" is our witness of Him using us to bless others; "see" is also the visual eye candy of His creation and the love we witness in people during our travels.

As you seek God's apparently elusive will for your life, consider this: There are a series of published children's puzzle books that have been on the market for several years. The books are filled with illustrations depicting dozens or more people doing a variety of amusing things at a given location. In each illustration, young readers are challenged to find a specific character hidden in the group. As you read *A*

*Call to Inspire*, we challenge you to find the divine character aspect of each experience. We pray that doing so will ignite a spark of interest for you to discover God's will in your everyday life.

> The Holy Spirit is somewhat like a compass. If we follow Him, He will always lead us in the right direction . . . Walking in the Spirit requires that you respond to His leading. You must allow the Holy Spirit to determine and direct all of your activities.
> —Dr. Lewis W. Gregory, *Introducing the New You*

Andrew Parkany age 15

One of the author's grandchildren was inspired to capture the image of the book's subtitle - "Bridging the chasm between God's will for our lives and ours".

# *Divine Appointments*

Since the Spirit of God was sent not only to be studied but
ultimately to be experienced, it seems to me we have stopped
short of God's intended purpose if we merely discuss and debate
His presence instead of exulting Him on an intimate basis.
—Charles R. Swindoll, *Flying Closer to
the Flame* (Word Publ. 2003)

# Captured at Leesburg Falls

Linda and I both share a passion for traveling the byways of the USA. Sometimes, our travels include visits with relatives. In the fall of 2009, we departed Connecticut, our home at the time, for a visit with an aunt and uncle who lived near our hometown in Western Pennsylvania. We had a unique camaraderie between us and Aunt Phyllis (now deceased) and Uncle Steve. Being with them was always a delight.

Typical for our visits home, we joined them on another local day-trip. After stopping for lunch at a country tavern, we drove several miles through the rural countryside. To my surprise, we arrived at the strangest location for a jewelry store. The store was owned and operated by a well-respected area jeweler, a former business acquaintance and friend of my Aunt Phyllis. I was puzzled. Normally, one thinks of a jewelry store in a mall, a plaza of shops, or on a main thoroughfare in town. Well, this store is a far cry from that image. As we drove into the parking lot, large Grand Opening signs peppered the landscape off the rural road approaching the store—notice I didn't say highway—and my curiosity grew.

The grand opening festivities were to begin shortly in the parking lot. Local media and county government dignitaries were everywhere. We chose to go inside the store. Aunt Phyllis and my wife were eying up the jewelry, while Steve and I began talking with one of the male sales associates. My first question obviously was *Why this remote location?*

It turns out that many years earlier, the owner became enchanted by the beauty of the waterfalls that graced the edge of the existing property high above the stream below. The stream is bounded on the east side by a Pennsylvania State Forest and the west by private land owned by a farmer. The owner had more than once approached the farmer with an interest in buying the property but was unsuccessful until 2007. The jewelry store owner's dream was to relocate his successful suburban retail store to the top of the glacial gorge overlooking Scollard Run and in view of the fifty-feet-high Leesburg Falls. Being a fan of architect Frank Lloyd Wright, the owner wanted his new store to be made using stone found on the property so as to blend organically with its natural location. The store goes by the owner's name but is known widely and appropriately as Diamonds by the Falls. The store was built on the edge of a chasm just below a waterfall. Leesburg Falls was one of Mercer county's special natural attractions. Though remote, the surrounding area was becoming a popular tourist destination with quaint shops and also an outlet mall that was bringing visitors from Cleveland and Pittsburgh some sixty to eighty miles away on a regular basis.

Shortly after purchasing the property and beginning construction, the owner was approached by archeologists from nearby Youngstown State University (YSU). The archeologists told him that buried beneath the rubble below the site for his store was an old iron furnace. Western Pennsylvania and Eastern Ohio had deposits of iron ore and beginning in the 1820s, many water power-enhanced furnaces began crudely producing iron. With the owner's permission, the archeologists unearthed the old furnace and the site is now historically preserved. Artifacts uncovered in the process are on display. In the beautifully designed store hangs a very large artist's rendering of what the furnace site looked like when it produced iron from 1820s to the 1850s.

The store salesman then told us that tomorrow the archeologists will be here as they are every Friday, continuing their work. "The old iron-making furnace is completely unearthed," he said, "and they're continuing to uncover the surrounding area for historical purposes. You're welcome to come and watch."

Wow! This was an invite I would not pass up. I've always had a fascination for unearthing the past and now I had a chance to witness the process close-up. Early the next morning, I set out, inviting my brother, Jerry, to join me. His youngest boy, Jacob, aged eight was off from school that day and tagged along. It would be a unique educational experience for the three of us. When we arrived about 9:00 a.m., the archeologists were already busy.

The next two and half hours flew by too quickly. It was a short sleeve day with the sun peeking in and out of the clouds. We watched in fascination as the six archeologists worked busily at their trade. Perhaps a half hour went by when one of the female workers stopped her work to explain and describe the site to us. And she gave us each a piece of slag, a hard, greenish, glassy material, a by-product of the production of iron containing other minerals. "This is what the jeweler-designers are now cutting, polishing, and mounting in expensive jewelry, calling it by a new name: Ironmaster's Gem," she said.

"I discovered the new gem in the store yesterday," I said excitedly.

"I also discreetly purchased a pendant as a surprise future gift for my wife." Ironmaster's Gem is really unique in texture and color.

During the morning hours, I had taken all the pictures I wanted to preserve the memory of our visit to this historical location. Curiously, my brother wanted to stay a bit longer, so I found myself a rock to sit on and watch the archeologists at work below. I had a perfect, unobstructed view of the falls.

The water flowing over the falls was more than an autumn trickle yet far from what it must be in the spring when water tables are much higher. Still there's something magical about a waterfall. Both the sight and sound of it is healing to me. Mesmerized by the view and the exciting experience, I became somewhat oblivious to a young couple that suddenly appeared standing atop the waterfalls about fifty yards or so from where I sat. As I began watching them, I became somewhat curious about their purpose for being there late on a Friday morning. Suddenly, I was mysteriously prompted to photograph them.

Silently, I heard a voice say: "Start taking pictures of the couple." I know it sounds weird, but that's what happened. I listened to that still small voice and in just a few minutes, I had snapped twenty photographs of the couple, including the surprise capture of their engagement—him on his knees—using my telephoto lens. As they started to walk away, I realized that the photos I'd taken rightfully belonged to them, not me. I was merely an instrument of God in a divine process. That's what Linda and I had come to realize after experiencing so many experiences of divine providence during a journey west a two years earlier.

Presuming the couple was headed to their car and not knowing exactly where I was going, I began running up the long steep crude road from the gorge and around the store. From there I found a path leading upstream. Soon I caught a glimpse of the couple as they were about to enter their car. When I approached them, I was totally out of breath and they were surprised to see this guy in a cowboy hat toting a large camera running toward them, hollering "Wait, wait!"

As they smiled, still holding hands, I said, holding up my camera, "I just photographed your engagement. I believe God led me to this place and time just for you. My wife and I call them divine appointments."

She replied, "Praise God," and he said, "Amen."

*Wow*, I thought, *a Christian couple.* Still out of breath, I offered, "If you'll give me an address, I'll send the raw images to you. I can send them through email but you might want one of them to frame and you'll need the larger image to do that. I used a 12X zoom lens so I know they came out great. Hope you like them." They gave me a Pittsburgh, Pennsylvania, address and also a big hug, saying thanks, introducing themselves as Tara and Wray. I said, "Don't thank me." And pointing upward, I said, "Thank Him. I was just an instrument in His orchestra of divine harmony."

I intended to watch some archeologists at work below a remote wooded waterfall. God intended me to witness a young couple committing their lives to each other through the lens of my camera. That's how the engagement of Tara and Wray was "captured at Leesburg Falls"—a reality twist on the jeweler's store name Diamonds by the Falls. Every time I reread this experience, I get emotional with tears of humility. Only a loving God could arrange this appointment!

But this story doesn't end at the waterfalls. Once back in Connecticut, I downloaded the engagement photos to my computer, edited them a bit, included a photo taken by my brother Jerry, and transferred them to a CD. Then, using a software program, I created a DVD video to add music with the digital images. The song I selected to accompany the video was one that Wendy & Gil, our oldest daughter and son-in-law, chose for their first dance at their wedding fourteen years earlier titled "Love of a Lifetime," popularized by a group called Firehouse. I then packaged and sent the DVD video and CD to the Pittsburgh address the couple had given me. I e-mailed Tara and Wray that the package was on its way. I was satisfied and convinced that God was finished with me and this couple. Then came another surprise.

A week later, an email from Tara surprised us. Tara and Wray were pleasantly surprised by the DVD video. They even used some of my photos on their wedding announcement website. They loved the song "Love of a Lifetime" so much that they decided to use it as their first dance song at their wedding reception. And because "God brought you into our life through the divine appointment at Leesburg Falls," they said, "you can expect an invitation to our wedding in June." We did attend the wedding which was held at the chapel of Westminster College where Tara graduated, just a few miles from Leesburg Falls where they got engaged.

But the story doesn't end at their wedding either. Four years later, I had another divine appointment that led to dining with Tara and Wray in Pittsburgh. I was a last-minute replacement as a chaperone for our church's high school youth group on a mission trip called The Pittsburgh Project. I led a team of six, two boys from Iowa, two girls from Lancaster County, Pennsylvania, and two girls from our church, making home improvements. Our team also had a local technical expert, Aaron, a licensed electrician. On Monday, first day at the worksite, the home of a handicapped woman, Aaron arrived during our lunch break. After introductions, I struck up a conversation by asking him about his future. "I just graduated from Pittsburgh Theological Seminary," he answered, "and will become a chaplin at the VA hospital come August."

*Hmmmm,* I thought, *Pittsburgh Theological.* Then I realized that was the same seminary that Tara and Wray may be still attending. So I asked him: "Do you happen to know Tara and—"

"Wray," he interrupted me. "Know them very well." He smiled. "We've been joined at the hip all through seminary. Theologically, we are on the same page. Why do you ask?"

Another divine appointment! I didn't tell Aaron about the Leesburg Falls experience, but I hinted that there was something special about my meeting Tara and Wray and suggested that he ask them about it. My divine appointment with Aaron, though, did lead to meeting Tara and Wray once again when I invited them to join our church's youth group for dinner one evening. Their mission trip that summer was called the Pittsburgh Project 2013. What timing! Tara had just graduated and Wray had just accepted a call to a church in western New York. They were packing to head north together the following week. Praise God!

Is there more to this divine appointment experience? Only the one in charge—God—knows for sure. But believers know where it will end.

If you are not a believer, perhaps "Captured at Leesburg Falls" has also "captured" you in the sense that you may want to seek more information about a loving God who executes divine providence according to His will. If you are a believer, perhaps this story has "captured" your desire to know more about surrendering to God's will. In either case, *A Call to Inspire* has served its purpose.

> The Holy Spirit who inspired prophets and qualified apostles, continues to animate, guide, and comfort all true believers.
> —D. L. Moody

# Image of a Girl

*Why do we have to move? I don't want to move. All my friends are here.* Those were the thoughts that immediately came to mind and expressed when my parents told me we were moving to a neighboring town. And I repeated those words to my parents many times.

I had just completed the tenth grade and was devastated. Tears upon tears did not change the fact that my parents were buying a new home in an adjacent rural community called Hickory Township. Even worse, I would be leaving my best friends and schoolmates for the last ten years. It was as if my heart were being ripped out of me.

I loved our home and neighborhood in Sharon. Sharon was the largest city and primary business mecca in Mercer County in Western Pennsylvania. When my parents told me their reasons for moving, it didn't make the move any easier for me. "Linda, our house needs too many repairs and the neighborhood is deteriorating," my parents informed me to my dismay.

I called my best friend Janie, who lived up the street to tell her the news. I recall vividly, as if it were yesterday, she came running over and we sat on the bay window seat in the dining room crying buckets full of tears. "You can come and live with me," Janie said between sobs. I knew that would never happen. I just felt angry. I felt hopeless as a non-swimmer fallen overboard without a life jacket. Life as I knew it was ebbing away.

The saddest summer of my life ended in August 1962 at our new address—1435 Wakefield Drive. In September, I rode a bus for the first time to a new high school and was late arriving. In my ten years of walking to school in Sharon, I was never late. My first day to Hickory, I was late because of the bus. Not a good start!

I slowly made friends in my new neighborhood and at school. On the bus, I usually sat with a neighborhood girl named Kathy and another new friend outside of our neighborhood named Frani. Little did I know then that meeting Frani was a divine appointment.

We had about a twenty-minute ride to school so there was plenty of time for chatting. I don't remember many of our conversations, but I know one of our favorite subjects was boys—who was our latest crush?

One morning, Frani was excited to tell us about this new boy she had met. He worked at a drive-thru dairy product store on the Pennsylvania-Ohio state line where she had gone with her Mom to buy less expensive milk. Each week she would be anxious to see him and eventually they exchanged phone numbers. During those calls, she discovered many details about this "handsome blond boy" and shared them with us. He lived in a two-story yellow house on Grant Street in Sharon. There was a wooden fishing boat trailered in their driveway; he graduated Sharon High in 1961, was commuting to Youngstown University, and majoring in engineering. He also had a much younger brother. Every day, Frani had more details on this "gorgeous hunk." Frani seemed helpless to *not* talk about him.

Kathy and I had no boy interests at the time so we enjoyed her enthusiastic romantic dialogue and looked forward to hearing the latest updates. Finally, the "hunk" asked her for a date to go ice skating. But before the date took place, Frani had an untimely accident and broke her leg. After that, Frani said they never dated and their relationship, sadly, faded with time.

After high school graduation, I entered our local hospital's school of nursing in September 1964. The school had a three-year diploma program and the first nine months were crammed with the academics. To say it was a tough nine months is putting it mildly. We started with eighty students in September and by June there were only fifty left for the capping ceremony. Back then, nurses wore caps and it truly was an honor to receive your cap.

We had a short break after receiving our caps so I was glad to go home and unwind with my family. My first night home, I received a call from one of my good friends, Jeri, from my hometown of Sharon. She said the gang—her and four other girlfriends I knew well—were going bowling and wanted me to join them. My response was no. I was totally stressed out from nursing school final tests. My mom, however, overheard the conversation and strongly encouraged me to get out and have some fun with my friends. So I immediately called Jeri back. Little did I know then how motherly advice could be so divine.

Jeri, Janie, Jeannie, Sally, Mary, and I were well into our bowling when these two fellows came over to talk. The first fellow that spoke—Paul, I later learned—had a keen interest in Jeri and he somehow knew she was going to be at Hickory Bowl. He had called a friend to join him on the pretense of going to play pool.

When he introduced his friend, Ken Parkany, I couldn't restrain myself. I finally got to meet the boy Frani couldn't stop talking about. So I shouted, "Ken Parkany, *the* Ken Parkany, the *famous* Ken Parkany," in quick repetition! My comment caught everyone by surprise, especially Ken.

Later, in between my turns at bowling, I went on to dazzle and intrigue him with all the information I knew about him. I really wasn't flirting, though it appeared so. I was just so excited to meet this mysterious "hunk" who up till now had been the romantic interest of my school bus friend, Frani, three years earlier. I couldn't resist teasing him. Ken was totally clueless as to how I knew so much about him. Before leaving the bowling alley, I broke down and gave Ken the revealing clue—Frani.

Evidently, Ken thought I was seriously flirting with him and he somehow found out my phone number, called that week, and asked me if I'd go out with him. I accepted. From that first date until we were engaged two years later, I began to learn some surprising facts.

One thing I learned was that Ken and Paul did not hang out together. When Ken got a call from Paul, Ken was surprised, had no other plans for that Memorial Day evening, and agreed to play pool at Hickory Bowl.

Another fact was that Ken told Paul after leaving Hickory Bowl the night we met, that I was the girl he was going to marry. "It wasn't just idle infatuation," Ken said to Paul, "I was mesmerized by her bubbling enthusiasm, and gradually saw the image of a girl I hoped to marry materialize in front of my eyes. I had a warm fuzzy feeling. You might call it love at first sight, but something inside me convicted me of my decision."

Two and a half years later, we were married in October 1967. Fifty years after that and three families and twelve grandchildren later, we celebrated our golden wedding anniversary in October 2017. Though we've had some rough times health-wise, our lives together have been filled with many blessings.

So let us now rewind a bit and return to my high school days. Looking back to my extreme distress in moving to Hickory, I realize that the move was all part of God's greater plan. Ken, I learned, had changed from a part-time job in a supermarket to a full-time evening position at Ohio Milk Sales where he then met Frani. My family moved to Hickory where I met Frani. Ken accepted Paul's invite even though they had only met a couple times. My mom had strongly encouraged me to overturn my decision and go out with my girlfriends. There are other dots that could be divinely connected, but as the saying goes: "The rest is history."

In this seemingly puzzling series of events in the lives of many people, do you not wonder and recognize a divine aspect? Was it all coincidence, chance, fate, or the universe in divine harmony? You decide.

As Christians, we believe God's divine appointments are a fact of his will for our life.

# Field of Dreams

This field, this game, is a part of our past. It reminds us
of all that was once good, and it could be good again. Oh,
people will come. People will most definitely come.

—From the movie *Field of Dreams*.

## Tuesday, May 15, 2007, Dyersville, Iowa

My passion as a kid was baseball. A bat, ball, and glove were in my
DNA. It was the 1950s and baseball was America's sport.

My heroes played in the majors for the Cleveland Indians. My
dad was an Indians fan and like father, like son, I guess. My hometown of Sharon, Pennsylvania was a mere hour or so drive to their
stadium in Ohio on the shore of Lake Erie. I attended many games

there with my Dad, usually three or four times a summer for a four-game weekend series. We'd stay with my Mom's sister, Pauline, or Aunt Pinky who lived on Cleveland's east side.

Little League Baseball became the catalyst for my boyhood vision to play professional baseball. In my teens, I played in the Babe Ruth League. I also played for our church softball team. My love for the bat, ball, and glove sport never waned until I entered college in 1961. The major reason for my loss of interest in baseball at that time was due to a player's strike over salaries which negatively affected me. Also, my need to work full-time evenings while taking a full class load during the day eliminated any plan to try out for the college team; and I also realized that my diminutive five-foot, six-inch, 135-pound frame was far from professional material. While I let my dream of playing professionally wane, my passion for baseball did not die—it just went dormant.

This dormant passion came to light as we entered Iowa that fateful day in 2007. We were heading back to Connecticut during our first "Awedyssee"—a three-month journey on the byways without a schedule. I recalled that one of my all-time favorite movies, *Field of Dreams*, was made in Iowa. Every time I watched that movie, it ignited the passion I once played with as a kid. A quick stop at a visitor's center in Des Moines directed us to a Dyersville, Iowa.

Long after the movie' release in 1989, this diamond is strangely more precious to more people than any authentic baseball stadium in the world. Millions have been and are still drawn here from all over the world. The promotional brochure explains:

> If you build it, they will come. People have come from all corners of the world. People who are magically drawn here for reasons they can't explain. It exudes everything that is wonderful, the relaxed place, the pastoral setting, the rich history. The best thing about the place is what isn't here—instead of providing images and dreams, it is content to be a mere stage. It falls to each individual guest to supply whatever drama

and whatever cast he or she desires. True to the simplicity and pristine quality that made the film so endearing, the "Field of Dreams Movie Site" and all who visit benefit by the property remaining as it originally intended and so well depicted in the movie.

Today, I would relive a deeply buried dream. We approached the location slowly from a long distance off the highway. I stopped to gaze, letting my dream formulate, percolate, and simmer before driving further to the oversize empty parking lot, except for one other vehicle. The first thing I noticed was it was just like the movie scene, except for the makeshift little red gift shop away from the field that could be another farm building. This is a place that attracts millions of visitors and today I would have the magical diamond surprisingly to myself. Drawing from the well of my memory caused emotional tears to fill my eyes. This was a special moment for me. We walked over to the visitor's booth and bought some souvenirs, including a ghost-players jersey.

It was May, but with the cold north wind that forced the American flag to wave proudly, an angry overcast sky, and temps in the low forties, it felt more like March. Yet, the environmental factors really didn't matter. What mattered was that the movies' "ghost-players" and I were here alone, or were we? Out of a corner of my eye, I saw something I hadn't noticed earlier. A young fellow was walking off the diamond with a fairly large camera in hand.

As he walked toward us and was preparing to leave, I walked up and asked him if he would like to be in some photos, since no one else was there to capture him and the location together. I knew exactly how he felt. How could anyone come here without having a memory of them on this magical diamond? Would that be like knowing you won the lottery but misplaced the ticket?

A huge smile grew on this young man's face—noticeably Asian. He quickly reached into a bag and took out a baseball jersey—"Takasaki" blaring across the front. He had brought the shirt with him from Japan. It was his high school baseball jersey that he wore fifteen years earlier. He said, "This was a moment I wanted to capture from thousands of miles and many years away." He told us that he successfully applied for a temporary job assignment at General Electric in Cincinnati, Ohio, a day's drive away from Dyersville. I donned my souvenir jersey and Linda then photographed us with both his and our cameras. Today was the only day he had to travel here and fulfill his lifelong dream of having his photo taken wearing his high school baseball jersey on the "Field of Dreams." Like most other visitors, including me, he brought his own dreams with him from Japan. Yet no one else was there until we arrived. We felt blessed that we were there at that moment to help him fulfill his dream. We said our goodbyes. And then we stopped to pray, praising and thanking God. The Field of Dreams now had a new meaning to me!!

For the next half hour, Linda photographed me all over the Field of Dreams—in every position, and even running the bases for an imaginary home run. I had come full circle from seeing the movie to actually being there on its stage.

Reflecting on this experience, we found ourselves near the "Field of Dreams" due to severe weather issues that diverted us into Iowa on an unplanned course. It was a divine intervention that took us where God wanted us to be. As I decided to fulfill my dream of visiting the magic diamond in Iowa, God, we discovered, actually intended us to take photos of a young foreigner who came to America on a temporary work visa, during his only window of opportunity to fulfill his lifelong dream!

For us, it was another in a long series of humbling experiences. This was also another example proving that God often provides vertical help through horizontal means.

# God Arrives at the Zoo, Finally

In April 2007, after a month of wandering the byways through the southwestern United States, our "Awedyssee" as we called it, led us to a destination where we planned to linger awhile. Awedyssee is a play on the word Odyssey, meaning to wander, where the "awe" was God-inspired events and "see" was witnessing His blessing upon us and others. Up to this time, we had several humbling divine appointments. "Would they continue if we lingered awhile?" we wondered.

San Diego was our home for three years in the mid-1990s. My employer, Pratt & Whitney Aircraft, a leading manufacturer of commercial and military jet engines reassigned me to a position there. I retired in 2004, and we had always looked forward to visiting again and to reminisce at our favorite places. We fell in love with the mild, mostly unchanging constant climate and sunny skies near the coastline, the friends we made, and of course the famous places like the San Diego Zoo, Balboa Park, LaJolla and its sunsets, and Old Town where we sipped tourist Margaritas. We also began to enjoy hiking the desert, a radically foreign experience to easterners. Living there had so affected us that once we were back east, our brains would occasionally and unpredictably upload a lingering memorable image. Linda or I would then say to the other, "Guess where I am." And that went on for quite a few years.

Of all the many fun places in San Diego, the zoo was Linda's favorite. As residents, we had an annual membership. Since the daily adult gate fees for two were half the cost of an annual membership, it was a no-brainer to purchase the annual membership—with unlimited visits and many other cost saving benefits. Since we planned to make multiple visits during our extended stay, we purchased an annual resident membership, allowable since we were permitted to renew our former membership. This surprising and significantly cost-saving purchase resulted from a divine appointment conversation Linda had with a zoo representative near the ticket booth. Linda was ecstatic. And we visited the zoo every day. But little did we know then, we were in for an even bigger surprise.

The annual membership came with many benefits—free entry passes, food discounts, and discount bus ride passes—all benefits we would not use. With all that God had done with us and for us up to this time, it seemed natural to ask Him to lead us to someone who could use them. We met many people during the next nine days, none of whom could use the membership benefits. Even when we visited our former church, we did not find anyone to use them. We kept praying, confident that God did have someone in mind. But we were nearing the end of our San Diego stay!

Finally, on our last day at the zoo, I recall thinking many times throughout the day, *Lord, we know you have someone special in mind and we're leaving the zoo today for the last time. Just thought I'd remind you, Lord.* Our last zoo visit ended about mid-day. As we walked out the exit gate, I stayed behind, looked up to the sky and repeated my reminder to God, only this time aloud.

I then looked ahead of me and saw Linda approaching a young couple with five young children including two in a stroller. As I neared them, Linda offered them our freebies, but they were naturally suspicious. But when Linda explained that we just wanted to give them all our free passes, no strings attached, the young mother broke down and cried. Her husband said they lived near Los Angeles and wanted dearly to take the kids to the San Diego Zoo for the first time and they were really tight on money. "The reason my wife is crying," the husband said, "is that she prayed earnestly this morning asking God to provide. And now you two come bearing the gift she prayed for."

I immediately spoke up saying, "We're from Connecticut and halfway through a three-month journey without a schedule on God's time. We lived in San Diego in the mid-1990s and just spent ten days here. Through an earlier divine appointment with a zoo representative, we were able to purchase a resident annual pass with all these free benefits. Since we could not use them, we prayed for God to lead us to someone who could. That's you," I said. "God has used us as His instrument during our travels," I added. "We began to call them divine appointments."

We then introduced ourselves to Ray and Ruth and gave them one of our calling cards. We pointed out that our email and travel blog site was printed on the card. "The blog site has daily entries that describe our prior divine appointments," I said, "and we'll be adding this one."

We hugged. Praised God, said a prayer for them, and then parted. About two weeks later, while in Arizona, I was checking emails. "Linda," I shouted. "Come here, you're not going to believe this. The couple with the five kids we met at the zoo, Ray and Ruth, here's an email from them." And it read:

> Hey Beeba and Papa, (our grandparent nick-names on the calling card)
>
> Ruth, myself and my children just wanted to thank you for blessing us with those free zoo tickets a couple of weeks ago! The kids had a blast. We were able to take the tour and saw a magnificent black panther in motion. We went on the skyline and the view for the kids was breathtaking. We saw and enjoyed so many of God's creation. The amazing part about it all is how our God so cared for us through you. That morning before we came, we were fretting about the expense of having so many children and being able to afford the trip as we found our-selves running out of money. We had cried out to the Lord that morning for His provision so when you approached my wife she was brought to tears at how an all-powerful God took time out to care for little oh us! Thank you for being Christ's hands and feet on our behalf. We felt His touch through you in a very real way. Thanks again. (Ray and Ruth)

It isn't often that we receive confirmation of our blessings. Their email naturally brought us to emotional tears. We keep in occasional contact today on social media. Ray became an ordained pastor and church planter. Do you see how two simple prayers by two couples far apart came together? Linda and I intended our visits to the zoo to be reminiscent of the years we lived as residents of San Diego in the mid-1990s; but God intended it as a way to also show His Grace to a family in financial need who prayed, trusted Him to provide and then for both them and us to patiently await His timing.

# From Promised Land to Promised Land

Promised Land, Pennsylvania, May 4, 2018—I'm sitting on the rear porch of a cozy cabin set back a hundred yards from Pennsylvania byway Route 390, perfectly perched at the edge of a wooded area and a wildlife corridor. The sun has sunk below dark clouds on the western horizon, its dim light barely visible. A severe thunderstorm watch is in effect for this Pocono Mountain region until 2:00 a.m. The wind is already unsteady and increasing in intensity, periodically gusting with a howl that increases and ebbs like the tide. The trees in view are mostly oaks, large but naked, yet allowing my vision to reach deep into the forest. Fallen tree branches and rotting logs dot the forest floor still paved with last year's fallen oak leaves.

Linda has joined me. As the sky darkens, our heads turned from one side to the other, as we wait for a repeat of last evening's arrival of white tail deer and black bear. For thirty minutes last evening, we watched one black bear, estimated to be four hundred pounds, just a few yards from where we were sitting a bit nervously around a campfire. Is it just a coincidence that we're in what many call God's country, Promised Land State Park? We may be here as temporary inhabitants of God's wildlife territory, but He arranged this event many years earlier.

Darkness is encroaching. The wind is howling more frequently. We can hear thunder in the distance. Our hosts, Ruth and Bruce Miller, who celebrated their fiftieth wedding anniversary last fall, join us. Ruth and Linda decide to sit on the swing behind the cabin and light Tiki torches to keep away the black flies. Bruce and I sit on the porch sipping a cool drink. The four of us are watching and waiting for the deer, or if any of the four different size bears, nicknamed Booboo, Bubba, Theodore, or Goliath, will come to visit as they did at different times last evening.

Suddenly, as if appearing out of nowhere, three doe approach and begin dining. Two bright flashlights illuminate them as Linda snaps iPhone photos. Two trail cameras installed nearby are also snapping candidly every five seconds. This is a brief encounter for Linda and me. For the Millers, this experience repeats itself daily.

Their small but cozy cabin getaway is named Camp Dora, after Ruthie's aunt. Their purchase one year ago climaxed a lifetime of outdoor enjoyment. As lifelong residents of Northampton, Pennsylvania, an hour and a half drive from Promised Land State Park, they feel home again where their camping experiences started even as kids long before they met and married. For the past twenty years, they spent weekends and vacations in an RV park in Delaware, an oceanside experience versus than the deep woods of the Poconos full of wildlife.

They've come full circle now to Promised Land and by our visiting them today, so have we.

Forty years ago, Linda and I decided to introduce our three kids, Brian, seven; Wendy, five; and Kimberly, two to tent camping. Promised Land State Park is a three-hour drive from our Connecticut home. We discovered it when taking our usual route along I-84 twice a year, making hometown visits to our families in Western Pennsylvania.

While we intended to try out a camping area new to us, God, it seems, intended for us to meet the Millers to suit His divine purpose. We arrived late on a Friday and seeing us struggling in the dark from the campsite next to us, Ruth and Bruce immediately stepped in to help. And the rest is history; we've been like family ever since. The Millers had a son and daughter Brian and Wendy's age, which also helped in bonding us together.

These past forty years, we've shared birthday and wedding celebrations and other joyous occasions like retirements; sadly, we've been to funerals together too; and we've had many visits to each other's homes. Making blessed memories together seems to have been in our DNA, and still is. But we know that God introduced us.

When we met the Millers, they and a neighbor, Wanda and John and Wanda's parents, George and Josephine, had formed a Christian gospel singing group and wore God's Family T-shirts when performing with guitars, banjo, and harmonica. God used them and their musical talents as His instruments to shine their light on others. We followed them to performances like groupies and hosted them when they came to entertain at our Connecticut church. While still part of God's spiritual family, parent responsibilities of growing teenagers eventually superseded their desire to entertain as a gospel group.

The Millers and we are as close—or closer than—blood relatives. How was it that two families on two totally different paths, career and otherwise, in two different but not even neighboring states would meet and become friends for life? Campers are known to be friendly folks. How many meet and grow together as "family"? Only a loving God could arrange such a blessing. When folks see us together and discover we're not related and ask how we met, we say, "We actually met in the promised land." What a joy that meeting became for both of our families.

Perhaps you've experienced a similar experience in your life? But do you acknowledge the One who made it divinely possible? Is it fate, coincidence, or the universe in divine harmony? You decide.

# Willis aka Billy the Kid

*Thursday, March 22, 2007, Ruidoso, New Mexico.*

This is a mountain playground and resort town nestled in the tall western pines at 6,700 feet elevation in South Central New Mexico. Ruidoso has a population of roughly eight thousand, which probably explodes at least an order of magnitude, judging by the number of log and other rustic looking homes when vacationers are driven there by summer heat. The highway through town is lined with shops and restaurants.

After getting our room and a dinner reservation at the Texas Club, we head uptown and parked on the fairly empty main street. As we are exiting our minivan, a man with a camera dressed in black skiing coveralls is standing in the road in directly front of our vehicle. He appeared to be aiming his small digital camera at something above, so I asked him if he wants me to move our vehicle so he can get a better shot of whatever he is shooting.

Well, that's how we met Willis. He approached and for the next five minutes, he shared some polite chat, did a magic coin trick, and then explained what he was really up to by running across the street to fetch some photo albums from his car. When he returned, the words blessing eventually came out in his conversation.

We then shared with him about our faith and also the many divine appointment experiences during our journey. Both Willis and we, it turned out, are of kindred spirits—both doing a ministry in our way using our spiritual gifts. Willis loves taking photos of people. The examples he showed us were of business folk, shop owners, entertainers, in touristy towns. He prints and frames the photos and then returns, sometimes a year later, to present the photo subject with his/her special photograph. To Willis, he's doing what comes naturally. His personality is so magnetic, energetic, and powerful, that you feel more special because he stopped to meet you.

I suggested to him that his hobby was a ministry. Willis said he never thought of it that way. He just likes to make folks smile or laugh. Willis said that, "Studies show children laugh hundreds of times a day, while adults laugh a few times, if at all." Back in Wichita, Kansas, Willis listens to folks tell him sad tales and his state department co-workers say "Willis makes all the customers smile." What a reputation. What a gem. We told him about our Awedyssee and that we felt a calling to make our journey a ministry and let the Lord do His thing.

Since we were in Billy the Kid territory, Lincoln County, I came up with the nickname for Willis aka Billy the Kid. First, because Willis's energy is like that of a kid—a very excited kid to boot—full of enthusiasm; second, because Willis has shot a lot of folks, albeit non-fatally through the lens of his camera; and third, because Willis travels a lot through the west and mid-west, something the notorious outlaw of these parts did; and lastly, because we met in Lincoln County, just up the road from one of Billy the Kid's famous hideouts, the old grist mill. Linda and I were very blessed to have crossed this modern Billy the Kid's path.

Later, he said he initially thought we were town chamber members because of our western appearance, there to welcome him. Though I didn't tell him, we initially suspected he was hired by the town to welcome strangers on the sidewalk. Neither of us was correct.

We certainly comforted each other and each of us expressed our Christian love. Beyond that, we don't know always know why we meet such strangers along our trail. But we also know that mystery is left up to the Holy Spirit. Though separated physically by more than a thousand miles, we've continued our friendship through the years, digitally.

So if you are traveling out west and you see a fellow with an infectious smile, camera in hand, and perhaps performs a magic coin trick for you, it just might be Willis (aka "Billy the Kid"). God bless you Willis in your ministry.

# Never Missed a Day

Do you have someone—a friend or relative—you can truly trust at all times, no matter the circumstances? Does that someone always have your back? Can that someone take care of all your needs?

On Sunday, August 21, 2011, the Katy Rail Trail in Missouri introduced us to a very unusual man, who then introduced us to his trustworthy friend. It happened at the North Jefferson Trailhead on the Katy Trail in central Missouri. The railroad symbol for the Missouri-Kansas-Texas Railroad was K-T, which affectionately came to be called the Katy Trail.

This was our second journey or Awedyssee as we called it, across the USA without a schedule or itinerary. We aimed to ride Rails-to-Trails bikeways as we wandered across the country. To date, we had logged over two hundred bike miles.

Linda and I arrived at the North Jefferson trailhead about 1:00 p.m. Immediately after parking, we noticed an eastbound rider getting off the trail. He quickly found the only shaded picnic table as it was baking hot in the mid-nineties. Both the rider and his bike were very unusual.

\* \* \* \* \*

Far from a Lance Armstrong look alike or even a casual bike rider, this rider was shabbily dressed in long baggy pants, old well-worn high-top leather military boots, a ball cap, and T-shirt that had seen better days. He appeared more like a homeless guy you might see on a city sidewalk, or, as Linda thought, a weary battle-scarred veteran of the civil war. He certainly didn't look like anyone we had seen biking on a rail trail. His scraggly short beard covered a rough-skinned face.

His bike was loaded down with four long, huge saddlebags that appeared to be made of cowhide skins that nearly touched the ground on both sides of his front and back wheels. There were some spare bike tires hanging off the back of the bike. This was not a comfort bike as we owned. In fact, we'd never seen a bike loaded down like this ever.

A sketch of Gary's bike by author Ken Parkany

We noticed that the man kept to himself as he prepared some food with a small well-used single propane burner he had fetched from one of the huge saddlebags. This apparently was not his first rodeo.

As we prepared to ride, our paths crossed with this unusual gent. We sensed the Holy Spirit nudging us and introduced ourselves. Just plain curiosity would not have raised my courage high enough to be nosy. Linda asked him where he was headed. "Pittsburgh," he said in a soft-spoken voice.

"Pittsburgh?" we repeated, "that's a long way east from Missouri."

He said he spent the past winter in Houston and this year he was planning to spend the winter in Pittsburgh. As we talked a bit and made eye contact, I noticed his eyes. They were the most dazzlingly brilliant blue eyes I'd ever seen, eyes that I'd never seen before. Yet the more I looked at him, the more his eyes appeared exceptionally confident and gentle, like someone old and wise. The strange thought of him being an angel whizzed quickly through my head. There was something strangely odd and lovable about him simultaneously. When we introduced ourselves, he said his name was Gary.

We could have asked a lot of questions but I wanted to avoid asking anything too personal. So I asked him how he was managing his long-distance travels. "Oh," he said confidently, lifting his head up a bit and aiming his eyes skyward, "He's been providin', never missed a day—not one."

*Whoa,* I thought, *this fella has a lot more faith than a grain of mustard seed.* What an example of surrendering! After some more back-and-forth conversation, I asked him if he could use some cash and when he said, "It'll help some," I reached into my pocket and picked out the largest I had—a ten dollar bill. Though I secretly wanted to linger, we said our goodbyes and said we'd pray for him and headed out eastbound on the trail.

During our ride, neither Linda nor I could get Gary out of our minds. Miles later, we discovered we were both thinking about him as we rode. Where did he get his faith? Did we really sense the Holy Spirit's voice? Should we have helped him more? Well, when we arrived back at the trailhead almost two hours later, Gary was still there and asleep on the picnic table bench. We moved our car into a shaded area. It was over 100 degrees now. We were sweaty and needed to rest a bit and get refreshed with some snack food before we began a second twenty-mile round trip ride westbound.

About fifteen minutes later, Linda noticed Gary sitting up, so she said she was going to give him some of the cold fresh Missouri peaches from our cooler that we got at the farmer's market in St.

Charles a day earlier. She then got some chocolate and some other snacks and proceeded toward him. When she returned, she said he couldn't take the bag of mixed nuts due to his bad teeth.

We then prepared for our ride but first stopped to talk to Gary again. While other bikers were avoiding him, I felt strangely drawn to him. When I queried him about his heavily loaded down bike, which I later regretted not capturing with my camera, he said that his other bike broke down on the Kansas section of the Katy trail. Someone gave him directions to a bike shop and the guys there took parts they had and welded him a heavy-duty bike to handle his load. I said something to the effect that we admired his faith and he was an inspiration. He just smiled and said, "God provides. He always does. That's something I learnt long ago."

"Are you a preacher?" I asked curiously. He just smiled again. "No," he answered with a smile in his soft-spoken voice. I had this strange feeling that I could learn a lot about my faith if I could spend more time with him, but we wanted to ride and Gary likely wanted to move on too. Not once did we see him approach anyone or look up to talk to any others walking by. Nor did we see anyone else approach him. He just kept to himself. He already had a friend—likely the only friend he needed.

Was it just a coincidence or the universe in divine harmony that a few hours earlier we listened to a Bible study on Luke Chapter 12. We attended Trinity Lutheran nearby and after the 8:00 a.m. service, a couple asked us to join them in the adult study. Included was the topic: Do Not Worry. Someone in the class read verse 22–31:

> Then Jesus said to his disciples: "Therefore I tell you, do not worry about your life, what you will eat; or about your body, what you will wear. For life is more than food, and the body more than clothes. Consider the ravens: They do not sow or reap, they have no storeroom or barn; yet God feeds them. And how much more valuable you are than birds! Who of you by worrying can add a single hour to your life[b]? 26 Since you can-

not do this very little thing, why do you worry about the rest? "Consider how the wild flowers grow. They do not labor or spin. Yet I tell you, not even Solomon in all his splendor was dressed like one of these. If that is how God clothes the grass of the field, which is here today, and tomorrow is thrown into the fire, how much more will he clothe you—you of little faith! And do not set your heart on what you will eat or drink; do not worry about it. For the pagan world runs after all such things, and your Father knows that you need them. But seek his kingdom, and these things will be given to you as well.

Meeting Gary was a most unusual divine appointment. I believe Linda and I were being taught an important lesson about anxiety. Do we worry? Do we have a friend like Gary? While we were on our second ride westbound, I couldn't get this odd-looking, gentle-minded bike rider with the brilliant blue eyes out of my mind. Gary had such strong faith in God and was so willing to admit it to strangers like us! I was still full of questions. I wondered what life experience Gary had that led him to surrender so committed to his maker. Or was there another explanation?

Sometime later, the Bible passage about entertaining angels came to mind. Perhaps it was because the experience with Gary was so odd, I don't know. But Hebrews 13:2 reads: "Do not forget to show hospitality to strangers, for by doing so some people have shown hospitality to angels without knowing it."

Seven years have passed since our meeting Gary in Missouri. I often wonder *Did he make to Pittsburgh as planned? Where is Gary today? Is he still riding Rails-to-Trails like a biking vagabond? Is his unusual custom-made bike still holding up? How many other riders have encountered and approached him as we did? And will our paths ever cross again?*

How many folks have you met in your life, that have left you with such an enduring spiritual impact, that their memory refuses to fade? If none, perhaps it's time to open your heart.

# Stranger Than Fiction

While traveling north from our new Georgia home in August of 2012, we made a brief rest stop on Interstate 77 in northern West Virginia just south of Charleston. On the way back to our car, a friendly gent asked us how we liked our Thule 1600 carrier atop our 2010 Subaru Outback. We were a bit cautious as we neared this stranger but told him that it had served us well during many thousands of miles travelling across the USA. He then continued to chat. From past experience, we know that lingering conversation might mean God was at work, so we both silently asked the Holy Spirit to reveal it to us while we continued small talk. Noticing our bikes mounted on the back, he told us he owned a cabin on a rail trail in southern West Virginia, the Greenbrier, and suggested we ride the trail if we hadn't already. "It follows the Greenbrier River for eighty-two miles," he said encouragingly. His comment then led to a longer chat about biking rail trails. No apparent divine appointment yet.

As we were about to part, I gave him our biking calling card that we often share with those who may want information on the rail trails that we ride. The card includes our email and travel web site, which includes photos of our rides. We have ridden and photographed thousands of miles of Rails-to-Trails bikeways all over the USA. When he noticed my words on the card, "There is no greater *joy* in life than to sense the Holy Spirit at work . . ." this stranger changed the subject of our conversation.

He then introduced himself as Ross and shared an amazing experience he had some years ago traveling like us across America. He travelled on his motorcycle and his travels were totally devoted to Bible reading, prayer, and winning new souls for Christ! "The

Holy Spirit led the way and I followed," Ross said smiling. Amazing! And we listened with great interest for fifteen minutes as he shared a few detailed experiences. We wanted to chat longer but he had a scheduled meeting north in Charleston. He encouraged us to try the North Bend Trail further north near Parkersburg. We hugged and parted but not before he told us about some great local churches should we return to this area. And then he asked if he could pray for us. He did so.

As soon as we got in the car, we looked at each other and Linda mused, *Wow, what a wonderful God.* We pulled off the interstate for a brief respite so God could arrange a divine appointment. Praise God. We then prayed, including blessings for our rest stop friend and his motorcycle ministry. During our North Bend Trail ride later, our thoughts were consumed by the divine appointment with a man that allowed the Holy Spirit—similar to how He had used us—to minister to others during his travels across the USA. This was a powerful confirmation and testimony that our divine appointments—Linda's and mine—were not unique. Praise God.

# A Beanie Baby Ministry

We arrived in the Connellsville, Pennsylvania parking area about 10:00 a.m. to bike ride a section of the Great Allegheny Passage or GAP, Pittsburgh, Pennsylvania, to Washington, DC. Connellsville is about thirty miles southeast of Pittsburgh. This was August 2011. We had recently closed on the sale of our Connecticut home and had placed our belongings in storage. With no new home to move into, we had decided to travel the USA for a few months, bike as many rail trails as we could find along our path and complete our journey in Georgia near our two daughter's families. We trusted that God would lead us to our next home somewhere near them.

As we were getting the bikes and gear ready for our planned thirty-mile roundtrip ride, another car pulled in with a young male driver. He paused near us and asked if this was the right place to park for the trail as there were no obvious signs. "Believe so," I replied, and he pulled in beside us. He got out and I walked up to introduce myself and handed him, Dave was his name, one of our calling cards and mentioned our planned journey across the USA over the next few months. If he followed us on our website, he could learn of new trails, including some of the Hall of Fame Rail Trails and may be inspired to travel west to ride them as well.

When he read our calling card, he noticed my mention of the Holy Spirit, and then asked if were praying for people as we travel. What got his attention were my words "There is no greater joy in life than to sense the Holy Spirit at work, for we are all instruments in His universe of divine harmony."

Dave said he was in need of prayers as he was in between jobs. "And my wife and I just moved out of Kentucky into southern Ohio, and we don't know a soul there," he added. "Can we pray?" I asked? So Dave, Linda, and I held hands in the parking lot and I prayed. He thanked and hugged us and went to his vehicle to prepare to ride.

Then Linda looked at me and mouthed the letters *BB*. I knew immediately what she meant. She went to our Subaru Outback to retrieve several Beanie Babies from a collection we brought with us. The Beanie Babies belonged to a deceased friend who, for twenty-seven years up to her death, was paralyzed from the nose down with spinal muscular atrophy (SMA). Her name was Ashlee. She became fascinated with the variety and colors of the stuffed animals, so friends and relatives kept adding to her shelved collection. My wife Linda was one of Ashlee's private duty nurses for nine years and we became close friends of Ashlee and her family. I was honored that the family even asked me to speak at her memorial service.

Following Ashlee's death, her parents came to us and gifted us with about fifty Beanie Babies, all different. "We know from your prior journey across the country," her Mom said, "how God used you to bless so many people. So on this new journey, we will pray that God leads you to someone who needs some TLC (Tender Loving Care) and when He does, please share Ashlee's inspiring story with them and give them one of her Beany Babies."

That was a task beyond our capability alone. It would be all about trusting God to lead us to those people. You just don't walk up to strangers and say, "Hey, do you need some TLC?" But we would trust God, we told them, and grant their wishes.

Well, our journey could either be one of ending with all the Beanie Babies still in our possession, or an incredible adventurous journey of God's supernatural divine providence at work. After two weeks of traveling and biking rail trails, and meeting many strangers along the way, today was the beginning. Dave was the first one we were led to by God (or was he was led to us?), that approached us asking for some TLC.

We approached once again and shared Ashlee's story. Dave was amazed. At our offer of several to choose from, he selected the Cardinal. We mentioned to Dave how God had supernaturally used us four years earlier on a similar journey and prayed for the same on this one. "Apparently, Dave, He's doing it and you are our first divine Beanie Baby appointment." Dave said he now lives near Cincinnati, Ohio and when we told him of our plan to head that way, he invited us to contact him to ride on some trails in that area and we agreed if he emailed us, we'd certainly do so.

And you know what's interesting? Though Dave and his wife had just moved to Ohio from Kentucky, it's unlikely he knew that Ohio's state bird is—you guessed it—the Cardinal. Coincidence or the universe in divine harmony—you decide.

# God Completes His Task

At the end of October 2011, Linda and I completed a three-month-long journey, our Beanie Baby Ministry, across the USA. We ended our journey in Georgia and alternated staying with our two daughters' families, until we found a permanent home. The closing on the sale of our Connecticut home took place in July and our furnishings were in storage.

What made the long journey across the country so special was the Beanie Baby Ministry we discussed in detail in the previous chapter. For some mysterious reason, we had three of the cute stuffed animals left over and decided to take them with us on a new journey north to visit family. Perhaps, just perhaps, God had a special place for them?

It was early December when we departed Georgia for a ten-day visit with our son's family in Connecticut. As usual, we chose to break up the thousand-mile trip by traveling less than a day's drive to our hometown of Sharon in Western Pennsylvania. The morning before leaving Sharon for Connecticut, December 5, Linda decided to purchase some special chocolates at our favorite candy outlet, Philadelphia Candies, while I decided to get an overdue haircut. Using one of my cell phone apps to find Great Clips, I checked myself in just two miles from my uncle's home where we were staying. Linda dropped me off and drove to get the chocolates nearby.

Once inside Great Clips, Sheryl (not her real name), a midthirty-something gal sat me down and began her work after asking me my cut preferences. A conversation began with her asking if I was from the area. I said, "My wife and I are both from the Shenango

Valley but lived in Connecticut for forty-four years where we raised our three kids. This past July we sold our home, put our furnishings in storage, and spent four months on a fourteen thousand-mile journey across the USA on byways without a schedule. We also biked 630 miles on Rails-to-Trails bikeways. And now we are looking for a new home in Georgia near our two daughter's families and nine of our twelve grandkids." I then shared the all details of our Beanie Baby Ministry.

"Wow," she said, "That's some adventure. I'd love to take a long trip like that someday with my girls." Sheryl seemed sincerely impressed by our journey.

I added that if a gift of a Beanie Baby to folks in emotional need was truly God's vision, then we would have to trust Him. God would have to lead us to folks that needed TLC. "Be kind of weird to go around asking strangers if they needed some TLC," I said. "But you know what? God did lead us to them in His way and His time."

I didn't share with my haircutter that we had given away all but three Beanie Babies on our journey, an amazing testimony to trusting in God and His purpose. Linda and I were puzzled why we had three Beanie Babies leftover. If God is so perfect, why did we end up taking three out of fifty or so home with us?

I then asked Sheryl as she was finishing up, "And what about you?" She said she was born and raised in the area, gotten married, and had three young girls—seven, five, and three years old. She then shocked and saddened me.

"A year ago I came home from work to find my husband with my girlfriend," she said. "I have since divorced him and I'm really struggling now. I'm living with my mom, working two jobs, and with no car of my own, trying to raise my three girls."

I told Sheryl that I was very sorry to hear about her plight and would add her to our prayers. My haircut complete, we proceeded to the register. I gave her a generous tip saying, "Buy some candy or a treat for your daughters for their Christmas stocking," and said good-bye. But as soon as I left the building, I phoned my wife. "Linda, when you come to pick me up, get the three Beanie Babies out of the back of the car. God found them a home."

"All three?" she asked in amazement.

"Yes, you won't believe it," I said. "I'll explain when you get here."

We then walked into Great Clips together and asked for Sheryl. When she came to the counter, I introduced Linda who proceeded to take the three Beanie Babies out of a bag. The young mom got a little teary. Linda emphasized that the stuffed animals were not used. They had been shelved on display for Ashlee. We both said we hoped her daughters would appreciate them. She said they sure would and "I'll be sure to tell them about Ashlee."

We wished her a Merry Christmas, gave her a hug, and left praising and thanking God for completing a task only He could do—finding a home for every Beanie Baby we were given by Ashlee's parents before beginning our long journey five months earlier.

Some might find this experience unbelievable. No, we can't make up things that only God can create—if we let Him. It's just another example of the amazing grace of God.

What the word "inspired" meant to the author's granddaughter.

# *Divine Interventions*

Don't allow the chaos in your life to overshadow
your time with people, and don't allow the chaos in
your life to overshadow your time with Jesus.
—Chris Emmitt, Lead Pastor,
Mountain Lake Church, Cumming, GA

# The Saddle as Our Pew—Part 1

It was now mid-April and midway through our eighty-four-day journey in the Spring of 2007. Since our departure in early March, we had driven about seven thousand miles and logged a couple hundred miles on our bikes. Linda had also recorded numerous divine appointments in her journal and I in my Yahoo blog.

Traveling east from San Diego, we had no firm destination in mind. We had become visually acclimated to the Sonoran Desert of the Southwestern United States, yet the giant Saguaro Cactus up close and the distant mountain scenery backdrop was still breathtaking.

The byway we chose finally led us to a large community. Welcome to Wickenburg—the Arizona roadside sign read. A check of the AAA map confirmed we were about two hours northwest of Phoenix at the junction of routes 60 and 93. Wickenburg, we learned after a brief stop at the town's visitor center, was an old west town that still had not yet been tainted by much progress. Only a few buildings were two stories. Some of the businesses still had the look of the old west, even covered wooden "sidewalks" with hitching posts. Soon we discovered why. This is cowboy and cowgirl territory and the location of many public guest dude ranches. It's also home to the annual Los Caballeros Ride where each year, cowboy wannabees arrive from across the USA and ride and live in the desert for a week, while their spouses and children bask in luxury on the many Dude Ranches.

While walking through town, we spotted a western shop for cowgirls only—a rarity—and decided to drop in. The owner was there by herself. "Hi, I'm Patty, the owner." Patty appeared to be in her mid-forties, with attractive tomboyish looks that could stop even a blind cowboy dead in his tracks. We later learned she had moved west from Connecticut some years ago—"Loved the west and loved horses too much," she said. She also lovingly crafts one to two custom saddles a year. Noticing my cowboy hat, she asked, "You here for the Los Caballeros?"

"Nah, just passing through," I answered, "that is unless you know of somewhere we could go horseback riding on a working ranch, not a dude ranch."

"There's only one person in these parts that fits that description: Rosie."

Patty gave us Rosie's telephone number saying, "Now, you'll have to leave a message as she runs a cattle ranch herself with a few friends who come by to help when needed. The name of her spread is EFFUS Ranch, a little west of town."

"Great," I said with very grateful enthusiasm. "We'll find a place to stay and give her a call." "Good luck finding a place. Los Caballeros usually has all the rooms taken," Patty yelled as we hurried out.

We providently found a clean motel room—the last one—in one of those motels from the past that lined Route 66 in the 1940s. The room was all decked out in western décor.—perfectly comfortable. We got through to Rosie directly that evening on the first call. We assured her we were experienced riders and after inquiring of availability the next day, she replied, "You bet. Come on out. Be here at 9:30 a.m. I'm taking a retired gentleman on a ride. You can join us." She then gave us explicit directions insisting that we close the gates after we drive through."

Following Rosie's directions the next morning, Saturday, Linda and I were startled by what we saw on the gate and immediately looked at each other smiling. "Wonder what He has in store for us this time?" Right next to the words EFFUS Ranch was a large Christian fish symbol!

Three miles later on the barren dusty road bordered here and there by old weathered fence posts linked by rusty barbed wire and large Saguaro cactus, we arrived at another gate leading to what we later learned was headquarters. EFFUS Ranch looked like a scene in an old western movie. Years of the burning southwest triple-digit heat had taken its toll on the buildings, fence posts, and rails. Horses stood already saddled and tied, ready to ride near some tin water troughs. The few desert trees provided little in the way of shade. The small unimpressive looking bunk house, Rosie's residence, stood out from the rest of the buildings as it had some fresh paint. Though the sun was bright, the Arizona April temperature was a cool sixty degrees on the large thermometer hanging on a nearby shed. The most impressive sight was our host—Rosie.

Rosie greeted us with a smile and a soft-spoken voice that was both inviting and hospitable. Her tanned face had a glow that spoke volumes about her work ethic. The confident gleam in her eye said she was passionate about her life choice as a desert cattle rancher, which seemed to keep her very trim and fit. Rosie introduced us to her student, John, a retired communications executive, and her vacationing ranch hand, Laurie. Laurie is the daughter of a close friend of Rosie. She appeared to be in her late teens and it was obvious by her looks, attire and demeanor, that she shared Rosie's passion.

Rosie then introduced us to our steeds by name and asked if we had water in our day packs as we'd be gone about two to three hours.

We assured her we did. "The horses know the way," she said. "We're gonna take it slow, maybe a trot now and then." We climbed into our saddles and were about to head out when Rosie took off her weathered and well-used cowboy hat, bowed her, and said, "Let's pray."

The fish symbol on the first entry gate was obviously not just an indication of Rosie's faith. Here was an experienced rancher who knew her priorities and where she, her ranch, cattle, and friends stood in the grand scheme of things. We intended to go on a horseback ride. God intended to have us meet a special child of God. Or was there more?

Prayer ended, we headed out of headquarters. For the next three wonder-filled hours, the eye candy was indescribable. Desert cactus bloomed everywhere, majestic mountains surrounded us on distant horizons, blazing sunlight sparkled off the desert sand, and several old gold mine entrances captured our curiosity. My camera lens captured nothing less than a few hundred images along the trail but actually just a meager portion of God's handiwork.

During our ride, Rosie would take turns riding next to Linda and me, as a way of getting acquainted. By the end of our ride, we sensed a special connection with Rosie. It seemed difficult to part. Then Rosie asked if we'd be around tomorrow. "Please come to our little church tomorrow in Aguila, just a little further west from EFFUS. The Aguila Community Bible Church is right off Wickenburg Highway. You can't miss it. The service begins at ten. I'd love for you to meet some of my friends there."

We sensed something special about our first meeting. So we agreed to do just that and headed back to Wickenburg. We looked at our map to get our bearings for Sunday morning. "A little further west of EFFUS" was actually eighteen miles. Amazing how relative a short distance can be in the wide-open spaces out west!

Late that evening in the motel, I was up to my usual daily routine of uploading the day's photos to online albums and penning a few words about our day's experience on our Yahoo website blog I created for the family and friends to follow us on our journey. Suddenly, I found my thoughts rhyming about our ride instead of journaling. The words kept flowing and I kept writing. When I was finished, I said, "Linda, you ain't gonna believe what just happened.

This rhyme just came outta nowhere or else God just had me write a poem—a cowboy poem. Nothing like this ever happened before. Let me read it," I excitedly began before she could say anything. "I titled it 'The Saddle as Our Pew.'"

I was in tears before I could finish reading the poem. "Where did this come from?" I thought out loud. "Why is God doing this?" I added. As I was thinking about what had just transpired, Linda said, "You should copy that on another piece of paper and give it to Rosie tomorrow. I think she'd love it."

I began copying what was apparently a divinely inspired poem. As I was doing so, the strangest, most bizarre thought occurred. Like someone was talking silently to me, I had the strongest feeling that I was going to read the poem to the congregation at church. It was a weird, very weird thought and chuckling to myself, I quickly tossed the thought aside.

Below is a photo we sent Rosie later that year. "Saturday April 14, 2007, EFFUS Ranch, Wickenburg, Arizona. Written especially for Rosie."

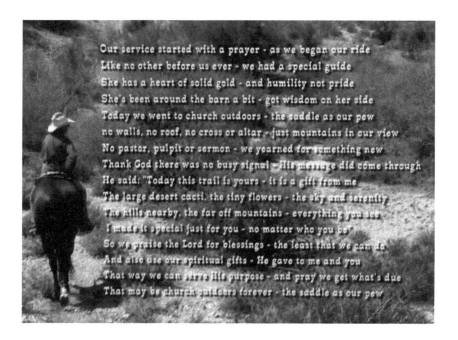

Our service started with a prayer - as we began our ride
Like no other before us ever - we had a special guide
She has a heart of solid gold - and humility not pride
She's been around the barn a bit - got wisdom on her side
Today we went to church outdoors - the saddle as our pew
no walls, no roof, no cross or altar - just mountains in our view
No pastor, pulpit or sermon - we yearned for something new
Thank God there was no busy signal - His message did come through
He said: "Today this trail is yours - it is a gift from me
The large desert cacti, the tiny flowers - the sky and serenity
The hills nearby, the far off mountains - everything you see
I made it special just for you - no matter who you be"
So we praise the Lord for blessings - the least that we can do
And also use our spiritual gifts - He gave to me and you
That way we can serve His purpose - and pray we get what's due
That may be church outdoors forever - the saddle as our pew

# The Saddle as Our Pew—Part 2

The next morning, Linda and I arrived early at the Aguila Community Bible Church, some twenty-five miles west of Wickenburg. Folks in the small church immediately noticed us as visitors and were very welcoming—all twenty attendees and all friends of Rosie, and hence, now our new friends. Rosie introduced us to everyone including Pastor Dan, a man in his late seventies and his wife. Pastor Dan, a retired pastor, and Sonja have been ministering to this congregation for several years. And Rosie is the worship leader.

Seeing a pretty female rancher dressed in a long brown flowing skirt, cowgirl boots, a western print blouse and scarf, who later began the worship service in praise song with such a heavenly voice, nearly startled me out of my boots. Here was Rosie, one day a desert cattle rancher in blue jeans leading a horseback ride, the next day an angel leading a worship service.

Next Rosie asked for prayer petitions from the congregation. Almost everyone piped up with one. Next Rosie asked, "Any praises today?" A long silence ensued. Unusual, I thought, and before I could raise my hand, Rosie said, "Well, I have one. Yesterday a man and his wife came to my ranch for a horseback ride. That was their intention. But God intended their presence for something greater. You see I heard God speak to me through them in a special way and I just want to thank Ken and Linda Parkany for coming to my ranch and for sharing their thoughts."

*Whoa,* I thought to myself, looking at Linda. "What did we say?" I whispered to her. Linda just gave me a puzzled look. Then Rosie asked for any other praises to be lifted up. Suddenly, my hand went up and I heard this still small voice say, "Read the poem." I then found myself standing and thanking Rosie for her kind words, making a brief comment about our three-month journey without a schedule, trying to be on God's time instead of ours led to many divine appointments—including Rosie—and adding that last evening, I had a very unusual experience. "Though I've been a freelance outdoor writer for many years," I said, "I don't find myself writing something quite like this"—holding up the poem—"and with your permission, I'd like to share it as a praise for Rosie." Heads were unanimously nodding affirmative.

Others, including Pastor Dan, said "Yes, let's hear it."

I then read the poem, words that came flowing from somewhere unseen the night before were now emotionally affecting those around me. By the time I finished, I saw amazement in the eyes of some, tears in the eyes of others. I thanked them all for allowing me to share those special words—words that were not mine I assured them—they definitely came from above. The congregation now knew that something special, something perhaps supernatural, had occurred between Rosie and us the day before. And all I heard was "hallelujah" and "praise God" over and over.

After a time of prayer, Pastor Dan began his sermon, and I got my pen and paper ready. I formed a habit many years ago of taking notes during a pastor's message. Knowing that the Holy Spirit can inspire their words, I knew that same Spirit may have words specifically addressed to me. But a very unusual thing happened. Instead of my usual note-taking, I found myself jotting down only a few words from the pastor's message. There were five words. As I looked at them somewhat puzzled, I noticed they didn't form a sentence or seem to make any sense. Yet I had felt a very strong urge to write them down when Pastor Dan was speaking and keep them. I folded up the note and put it in my shirt pocket.

After the service, the folks were hesitant to let us leave. They wanted to know more about us and our incredible journey. Rosie then invited us to brunch with some friends. She gave us the name and location of the place in Wickenburg, saying, "You linger awhile and meet us there," which we did.

Later at brunch, we sat next to Rosie. Her friends seemed like long-time acquaintances, not strangers to us. The camaraderie was uncanny. When we finished brunch, I said to Rosie that I was curious about the name of her ranch—EFFUS. "What do the letters stand for?" I asked. Surprisingly, she wasn't sure. She and her now ex-husband had purchased the ranch many years earlier and EFFUS Ranch was the deeded name, so they just kept it.

"Perhaps," she said, "the letters stand for the names of the men who first owned it? I honestly don't know."

At almost the same time, a strange thought came to mind—the words I jotted down during the sermon. I had the paper in my hand, showed them to Rosie, and told her how unusual it was that I had jotted down only five words, rather than my usual lengthy notes. But look at these words. Just then a light bulb went off in my mind. The words could be arranged to read "everlasting faith for unsaved souls."

Suddenly my eyes were opened to God's message. "Rosie," I said, "look at these words. They match the letters of your ranch, EFFUS—Everlasting Faith For Unsaved Souls." Curiously, Rosie's eyes welled up in tears. Once she got her composure, she asked if she could use the words in her ranch brochure. I said, "Sure, Rosie, they aren't really mine anyway. They came from God during Pastor Dan's message. Why do you ask?"

"You know the man that rode with us yesterday? We'll, he's a retired owner of a public relations firm and in exchange for teaching him to ride, he is going to produce a new brochure for my ranch. I've planned for a long time to begin a ministry for troubled youth, by having them be around the horses, the ranch, and taking them on horseback rides. That's what I meant when I said this morning that I heard God speak to me through you and Linda to go ahead with my plans. Those words are perfect—Everlasting Faith for Unsaved Souls, EFFUS." With emotion growing once again, she concluded: "What an amazing God we have. And you are one amazing instrument of His."

"Praise God," I replied. Yet I was still completely unaware of Linda or I ever saying anything that might have been God's words to Rosie. I guess we're not supposed to always understand how exactly the Holy Spirit works.

Sadly, the time came for us to part—with a generous flow of bittersweet tears. Might we ever meet again this side of heaven? Yes, we have visited Rosie on three subsequent occasions and stayed at her working ranch helping out with all the chores and joining her on scheduled horseback rides. Though separated by over 1500 miles, we have become very close friends and both text and call each other frequently, like family. Yet even today, I reflect back on that divine intervention during a sermon with both shock and awe. Linda and I intended to make Wickenburg a whistle-stop on our journey through Arizona. But our loving God intended us to linger longer so that He might demonstrate His enormous power through His Holy Spirit. He served His purpose by using us supernaturally as His instrument to bless a Godly Arizona rancher named Rosie. Hallelujah!

Are you willing to let God interrupt your plans so that He can use you to implement His plans?

# A Gift That Keeps on Giving

Have you ever heard God speak to you? I know that question seems a bit unusual, but God, according to His own words, does speak to us through His Word (2 Timothy 3:16–17; Isaiah 55:11) and through events (James 1:2–5; Hebrews 12:5–11).

During a three-month long journey in 2007, Linda and I had an almost daily series of amazing coincidences happen to us, that we eventually concluded only a loving God could have orchestrated them. We experienced supernatural events with complete strangers that deepened our faith and theirs. And these experiences humbled us to our knees in prayers of thanksgiving and praise. Amazing, yes, but Linda and I began to wonder—could a prayer blanket play a role in all of the above?

Prayer blankets or quilts are made in variety of ways. Regardless of style, they are gifts of love usually meant to provide comfort in difficult times. That comfort is intended to ease pain, strengthen, heal, help someone through an emotional crisis, and even provide warmth and connectedness to the ones who fashioned and prayed over the created fabric. For Linda and me, however, our prayer blanket was different. Our church's Prayer Blanket Ministry, on which we served, completely surprised us with one prior to our leaving on a retirement-celebration journey.

Celebrating retirement is a much-anticipated event. For us it was more, much more than we expected or could have even imagined. We planned a three-month minivan journey in the spring of 2007. Our plans included a location—the southwestern United States. Our itinerary was not destination-oriented and we absolutely had no definite schedule. During our year of planning, we felt an unusual calling to ask God to use us as His instruments along our trail, to make our journey a ministry. We were prepared to serve Him as we knew how—musically—entertaining seniors in nursing homes. Yet we prayed and trusted God for an answer.

Christian author Phillip Yancey describes this as the 'house specialty' type of prayer, common in Asia. You trust the host (God) to decide exactly what to provide, versus the 'transactional' type of prayer, so common in America, asking for specific guidance or help in detail. What actually happened in answer to our prayer both surprised and changed us forever and, doubtless, those we met, or should I say, those we were led to meet.

On Sunday, February 25, 2007, we attended our church a few days before departing Connecticut. One of the first things I habitually do in the pew after praying is to review the hymns for the day. The last hymn, number 326, was totally unfamiliar to me—"Bless Now Oh God Thy Journey." I nudged my wife saying emotionally, "He's coming with us." She looked at me curiously. Then I read the first stanza which ended, "The trail is found in desert and winds the mountain round, then leads beside still waters, the road where faith is found . . ." This time, I nudged her harder while tears welled up in my eyes, saying, "Look at these words—desert and mountains—they describe where we're going. Unbelievable! I think God's answering our prayer. I believe He plans to use us."

Little did we know that different prayers lay ahead. Following the service in the fellowship hall was a large table with material cut for a fleece prayer blanket. The fabric had southwest colors with a print of cowboys and horses. Church members were tying knots of love on the prayer blanket and praying for God to be with us, comfort us, and provide safe travels. Amazing. This surprising gift of love concluded with our minister giving the blessing with all hands on the finished blanket. The blessing included the four stanzas of "Bless Now Oh God Thy Journey." Then one of the ministry coordinators read a prayer instead of the usual Bible verse tucked into the corner pocket sewn to the blanket, "A Cowboy Prayer." What a thoughtful, loving send-off. What a comfort to know that we would be taking prayers with us—tangible prayers—in the form of a prayer blanket. During our journey, we found those prayers answered many times.

Tying knots           Praying over the blanket

During our eighty-four days traveling, we experienced God's Holy Spirit like never before. At first, we were surprised by events we encountered. Soon we began to see a pattern developing almost daily. God was using us as His instruments. We had planned to serve Him our way entertaining those in nursing homes by Linda playing piano and me guitar. Yet we found ourselves doing God's work His way often, as we never once visited a nursing home. The magnitude of His presence along our trail was awesome; the magnitude of His presents, His grace, was humbling.

Friends, pastors and groups with whom we were later blessed to share our experiences said that we should write a book. Well, *A Call to Inspire* is our way of sharing some highlights of the 2007 and subsequent journeys, or Awedyssees, as we began to call them. Our purpose is to inspire the reader to want the Holy Spirit who is present in all believers, to let Him use them His way. Augustine, the famous Catholic Saint is quoted as saying, "God provides the wind, but man must raise the sails." Just how the Holy Spirit might use you is a mystery, knowing that His gifts are specific to each one of us. But we must act for Him to act.

The dictionary defines odyssey as a series of wanderings. Any wonder why we called it an Awedyssee? We did so to reflect the magnitude of God's presence—the awe, and the amazing beauty of His creation along every byway and our witnessing of His presence—the see.

Our Awedyssee started with a prayer blanket and ended with a new beginning. We intended our retirement celebration to be a sojourn without a schedule; God, it seems, intended it to become a ministry, a calling if you will, to inspire others to desire a closer personal relationship with Him. Could a prayer blanket be a gift that keeps on giving? What do you think? Life is a series of choices. Long ago we made a choice to begin a closer walk with our Lord and *A Call to Inspire* is just small token of His grace to us. Have you made such a choice?

# A Hymn Signals Divine Healing

I didn't know where I was when I opened my eyes, but I knew I was in a hospital bed. My first thought was, *Something serious must have happened.*

The window sill was lined with cards and flowers, my head and body ached, and my dear husband Ken was sitting at my bedside with his hand on my arm. *What happened? Where am I? I don't remember anything,* were other thoughts going through my head.

When Ken saw me awake, I saw tears in his eyes. He told me I had been seriously injured in a bike accident and have been in a coma for five days. And he had been at my side almost continuously.

Later I was told that I had also experienced some permanent memory loss. Fortunately, I still remembered my husband and family. Ken reminded me that six days earlier we had arrived at my brother Michael's cottage on Hyde Lake in upstate New York. He and his wife Dawnelle had purchased the property six years earlier with four other couples, hence the camp's name Hyde Five.

I knew we had been going there for summer vacations with Michael and his family for several years. We loved our times together at the lake. It was the perfect get-away for family bonding, fishing, and swimming. The cottage was located on a small lake near the Thousand Islands in a rural setting away from hustle and bustle of everyday life. We would sit in the Adirondack chairs overlooking the lake, sip early morning coffee, listen to the wild call of the loons and say, "It don't get no better than this!" Those words were inspired by Dawnelle's late father, Johnny. He used them frequently when he visited Hyde Five.

Ken then gradually updated me on events. This particular year, our youngest daughter, Kim, and her boyfriend joined us. Our first morning there, Ken and I were up early for a bike ride on the nearby rural roads. For the past couple years, we had been bringing our bicycles with us to ride on the country roads nearby Hyde Five.

"This past Monday at 7:30 a.m., July 25," Ken said, "a dog ran across the road and hit the front tire of your bike and I watched from behind as you were thrown over the handle bars. You landed on your head and lay there unconscious as I tried to stop the bleeding from your nose and forehead. A homeowner happened to witness the accident and called 911. A nurse going to work providentially witnessed the accident and stopped to help while we waited for an ambulance to take you to the nearest hospital here in Watertown, New York, thirty-five minutes away. Because I had a calming influence as you occasionally struggled to come to, the EMT's and hospital staff suggested I be at your side in the ambulance and during a whole battery of tests, X-rays, and MRIs. The doctor said you had a traumatic brain injury with internal bleeding. 'We'll just have to wait and see', he said, trying not to discourage me too much. They put you in ICU and you've been in a coma for five days."

*Wow,* I thought. *Guess I'm really blessed to be here, alive and awake.*

Ken then shared something truly amazing. Kim came to be with her distraught Dad that first day. In the evening, the med staff suggested they go for a walk in the neighborhood. As they were walking back to the hospital, they heard the Carillon bells of a neighboring church playing the hymn, "What a Friend We Have in Jesus."

They both rushed toward the church as the hymn has a special meaning for Ken since his childhood. He would awake whistling or singing the hymn at breakfast on Sunday mornings many times. Each time they would then go to church and "What a Friend We Have in Jesus" would be one of the hymns for the service. As they neared the church, the hymn suddenly stopped and when they got closer, they saw the church mysteriously darkened. Was someone actually in the church playing the hymn? They curiously wondered.

Back at my bedside in ICU, Ken was reading from a book he had just purchased at a used book store on our drive to Hyde Five, *Norman Vincent Peale, Words that Inspired Him* (Inspirational Press 1994). He thumbed through the book and happened to stop at a chapter on pain and suffering. The last two paragraphs of what he read were: "When pain strikes, we often ask the wrong questions, such as, 'Why me?' The right questions are, 'What can I learn from this?' 'What can I do about it?' 'What can I accomplish in spite of it?' Bring pain or suffering to the One who suffered for us on a cross and you will find 'what a friend we have in Jesus'." As Ken recalls, he got goose bumps, read it to Kim, and then said convincingly yet in tears, "Mom's going to be all right. Mom is going to be okay."

It took several years and a few miracles for me to heal from my injuries. Four years after my accident, Ken and I were attending a church conference healing service on the final day. As I stood in front of the minister, two amazing things happened simultaneously. As the minister placed his healing-oil-dipped thumb on my forehead, a guitarist began playing "What a friend We Have in Jesus" and a staff photographer snapped a photo of that minister and me.

Our amazing God had displayed His amazing grace once again. That photo remains on our refrigerator door as a constant reminder of His friendship and His power.

Looking back after all these years, I truly recognize the power of prayer and the trust we must place in God for all things, so they will always fit into a pattern for good. The day of my accident, I learned that Ken called our pastor, Paul Henry, who prayed with Ken on the phone. Pastor Henry then called Pastor Paul Luisi, who lived near the Watertown, New York hospital and visited my bedside and prayed while I was in a coma. A week of intense prayer was followed by years of prayers by many others—friends, family and church family.

Though I experienced some permanent memory loss, loss of my taste for over two years, which the neurologist said would not return if it lasted more than a year, and nearly constant pain, I gradually improved. My taste miraculously returned and the lingering pain diminished, allowing me to return to nursing until I decided to retire in June of 2006.

All those many prayers beginning at the time of my accident were answered each time with a simple reminder of what a friend we have in Jesus. I hope He is your friend too. If not, He can be. The decision is yours.

# That Still Small Voice

*Thursday, August 25, 2011, St. Joseph, Missouri*

We left Independence, Missouri yesterday after touring Pres. Harry Truman's birthplace and earlier enduring nearly two weeks of bike riding periodically in ninety-to-one-hundred-degree heat in Indiana, Illinois, and southern Missouri. Weather forecasts were calling for more of the same. Looking for a little relief, we headed further north.

On our way, as evening was approaching, we felt convicted to do something completely out of the ordinary, for some reason. We pulled into a Comfort Suites in St. Joseph, Missouri, instead of calling ahead as we usually did, for a reservation. This stop turned out to be a divine intervention. Paula, the receptionist at the Comfort Inn, told us not only did they *not* have a room, but all but one area motel was booked! Huh? Unbeknownst to us, the heavy rains that preceded us weeks earlier caused severe flooding over a large area. The floods brought in hundreds of FEMA representatives and contractors, a normal event in this flood prone region of the United States.

Had we not made this impromptu stop and continued northbound, we would have discovered the Interstate and byways were all closed for sixty miles due to the floods. Our only way into Nebraska and then proceed north was to cross the flooded Missouri River here in St. Joe. Otherwise, to proceed in our northwesterly direction, we would have had to travel east, north and then west, hundreds of miles out of our way.

So we immediately booked the only room left in St. Joseph, the Best Value Inn. The next day, we visited a couple western stores, the St. Joe Boot Company and the Stetson Hat Factory Outlet, two great discoveries (for Ken) that we found after booking our room! Hearing and then obeying that still small voice had saved us many hours and miles of travels and disappointments.

Why did we stop here versus calling ahead? Was it coincidence or the universe in divine harmony? You decide. We pray that you have divine interventions that will change your direction and perhaps your life in both a convenient and pleasant way.

# Ashlee Inspired Others Even After Her Death

In February 2009, Ashlee, the twenty-seven-year-old daughter of friends in Connecticut, died. Linda, my wife, was one of her private duty nurses for ten years. Ashlee amazingly lived twenty-six years beyond her life expectancy as she developed SMA (Spinal Muscular Atrophy) as a baby. All those years she lived on an artificial ventilator to breathe, learned to communicate with a variety of new technology devices, and inspired everyone who came in contact with her.

Soon after Ashlee's death, her parents arranged a memorial service at their church. Ashlee's mother asked me to speak at the service by reciting the famous poem "Dash," and suggested that I play my guitar and sing as well. "Ashlee loved it when you sang 'You Are My Sunshine' to her," she added.

Before going to bed that night, I prayed, "Lord. What are you putting on me?" When I awoke the next morning, I was convicted to start writing. When I finished, I discovered that the words I had written could be put to the tune of "You Are My Sunshine!" I titled it "Ashlee, A Child of God." The day before the memorial service, the pastor asked me to come and rehearse the poem *Dash* and the song at the church.

When the pastor heard the words of the song, he came to me and confessed that his prepared message was totally inappropriate. The words to your song so inspired me that I feel I must prepare a new message based on "Ashlee, A Child of God." And he did. It was a moving memorial to a child that God used to inspire so many people during her twenty-eight years—parents, siblings, friends, medical staff, and others. Though Ashlee could not move but one tiny muscle in the palm of her right hand that she developed and used to communicate with computerized devices, she literally touched the lives of others like no one else could.

If God can use a paralyzed child like Ashlee so powerfully, what more can He do with others more physically fortunate? Like, maybe write a song that inspires a pastor to rewrite his memorial message?

I've included the song here because Ashlee, even after her death, had a significant impact on her pastor and his message, much like her life had a similar impact on those who knew and loved her during her life.

### Ashlee, a Child of God
by Ken Parkany

(sung to the tune of You Are My Sunshine)

In memory of Ashlee Hazel Tompko, September 18, 1981–February 27, 2009, beloved daughter of James and Bonnie Tompko, and lifelong resident of Vernon, Connecticut.

Refrain:
I am much more than
My parent's daughter
I am much more than
What you may see
I'm not just another
Pea in a pod
I am Ashlee, a child of God

Verses 1–4
I may look diff'rent
I may look strangely
But I am normal

As I can be
For it is not
What's on my outside
I'm the heart inside of me
(Refrain)

When I arrived here
As God's gift to you
Some twenty-seven
Plus years today
The doctors said that
My life was measured
Not in years, but months or days
(Refrain)

I guess the doctors
They were mistaken
God said their decision's rash
For the time spent here
Cause you cared for me
Was a lot more longer than a dash
(Refrain)

My dash represents
All the time I spent
Alive here on this earth
Now only those who
Cared and loved me
Know what that dash was worth
(Refrain)

(Note: last verse was adapted from the poem "The Dash" by Linda
Ellis, which Ken, at her parent's request, read at Ashlee's memorial service.)

# The Mystery of Glorieta

Thursday, May 3, 2007, Pecos, New Mexico. What do we get when we trust in the Lord? Admittedly, trusting Him is almost impossible in today's culture. We're raised, most of us, to be the captains of our own ships, so to speak. Our educational systems and sports enterprises teach us to excel, be first. And when we succeed, we give ourselves the credit. The great American dream, whatever it is for most of us personally, it's all, sadly, about "me."

The Bible speaks of the last being first. Huh? The Rev. Billy Graham preached to thousands— turn yourself, your life, over to Jesus. What? Then Max Lucado writes a book titled *It's Not About Me* (Nelson, 2004). When we hear these words, most of us nod our heads in silent agreement. Then we turn our inner dial to the "me first" station. Yes, it's hard to trust the Lord. It's hard enough to learn to trust someone you can see—a friend, loved one, or co-worker. But trust God?

Linda and I have had more than few run-ins with trusting Him on our Awedysee (that's purposely miss-spelled). We have an itinerary with no schedule, except for a three-month window. We are over 9,000 miles along a trail with no definition. We have tried to leave ourselves open via prayer to His guidance. When He calls, we hope He doesn't get a busy signal. Earlier in our journey, a planned whistle-stop on our trail became a three-day adventure with an Arizona ranch owner who invited us to her church and inspired the bard in me to pen a cowboy poem, a tribute to her.

If this appears spooky, the word may be appropriate. It implies mystery. And God does mysterious things. Because we are not on His wavelength here on this planet, we have to accept His doings. It's called faith. Believe in what you cannot see and the reward of your faith will be to see what you believe.

Today, as we follow directions to our horseback ride, we see a sign Prayer Garden and banners on pole lamps blaring Bible quotes. Are we in the right place? It's called Glorieta, a two thousand-acre church retreat and conference center.

We meet our guide, sign the necessary release forms, and he directs us to the conference center to use restrooms. While there, we are then invited to stay here at the center for $49 per night so that we might attend the one-year anniversary of the Pecos Cowboy Church nearby. We're told our guide was one of the men who started it. We enthusiastically accept as we're on God's time and I always wanted to attend a cowboy church service.

Eventually, we mount our steeds and ride up a narrow canyon thick with junipers and Ponderosa Pines from 7,500- to 8,500-feet elevation along an old road that today welcomes a trail horse and makes trying to visualize anything with four wheels difficult to impossible. At times we're riding in the shallow creek. We sense our horses would rather keep their feet dry. Star and Pat, both boys, are typically obedient to themselves. The hills are steep on both sides. Occasionally, there's a small opening, some blades of grass on a small flat. We ride past a former saw mill to a small ghost town. We dismount. Our horses welcome the break as they munch grass. We wander around the old hotel foundation, we peek into a couple of mine shafts, and we welcome an out-of-the-saddle chat with our gracious guide. We do all of this under a sky so blue, the puffy white clouds stand out like beacons beaming a message: It's a picture-perfect day. And our camera captures over a hundred images for this riding experience.

Our guide is a retired Texas cattleman, quite spoken. His Texas drawl is as thick as his graying mustache. A handsome fellow, he could star in an old western. He confirms he's also one of the founders of the Cowboy Church in nearby Pecos. He knows a lot about these hills but admits there's still more to learn. A lot of history took place along the Santa Fe trail. Gold was discovered in Golden, New Mexico south of here. Prospectors came along the trail to find their fortune. The railroads replaced the foot, horse, and wagon tracks. The famous Route 66 came next. Yep, three hours of horseback riding for us, but years of memories too.

Today, much of the land is Santa Fe National Forest (NF) and Carson NF. It's where the Great Plains meet the Rocky Mountains; it's where both the lawless and law-abiding cowboys made their own legends; and it's where Glorieta was founded over fifty years ago in the Glorieta Pass. And one of the places where Bear Creek Adventures has trail rides.

After our memorable ride, we ask for a standard room but unexpected circumstances lead to us getting upgraded to a first-class room. Thank you, Lord, again.

The folks are special here. We are made to feel special. It's the place, I guess. The beauty of the surrounding mountains begs being special, but the staff and volunteers make it more so. It's a place where millions of guests have come to renew their heart, mind, and soul or just "physical and spiritual rest," the brochure states. And now we know why.

That's how an afternoon horseback that turned into a five-day adventure began. On Friday and Saturday, we visited Native American ruins nearby and hiked a mountain trail to Cave Creek where the creek actually enters and exit a large streamside cave. It was on this hike that we somehow experienced fresh mountain lion tracks and bear clawing on trees—the gooey sap still running—fortunately without any actual wild encounters.

Sunday morning, we pack up to leave, thank the folks at Glorieta for their memorable hospitality, and check out. Plan to head east right after church. That's our plan, anyway.

Cowboy church, rookie attendees discover, is worship followed by entertainment, a prepared hot meal, and afternoon rodeo. Many of the attendees are local cowpokes and they enjoy calf roping and barrel racing for a few hours. While the meal was being prepared, I recognized one of the female singers as a Nashville gospel singer. Myra Green concurred with my recognition of her when I introduced myself and she then introduced Linda and me to her husband,

Cliff. They invited us to sit with them and join them for the rodeo. I said we were anxious to head east as we'd been on a long journey and we already had a horseback ride turned into an exciting three-day adventure so that we could attend our first cowboy church. But Cliff and Myra insisted that we stay for a portion of the rodeo and we agreed.

During the rodeo, the blue sky and jacketless temperatures gradually changed to something more threatening. Myra and Linda went to the Green's car while Cliff and I donned warm jackets. Cliff suggested to me that we should postpone our travels for a day as we continued watching the calf roping. A half hour later, as the temperatures dropped further and the northeast sky darkened, Cliff repeated his suggestion again, this time inviting Linda and I to stay at their home for a night on the Glorieta campus. The rodeo was still going strong when Cliff and I decided to go back to their car as our comfort diminished. He then repeated his invite a third time. When we reached their car, he told his wife about his invite and our plans need to be interrupted due to foreboding skies. It would not be advisable to be heading east into Oklahoma and Kansas just now. Mysteriously, I began to believe him.

I said, "Cliff, God usually calls our name twice to get our attention. You've repeated your suggestion three times. I think God is speaking to us through you, so we'll accept." We had the most enjoyable time with Cliff and Myra that evening and with her father too. What we learned both fascinated and humbled us. Cliff and Myra quit their jobs five years earlier and started Green Ridge Ministries, otherwise known as Bible Alive Theater, where Myra sings and tells stories of women of the Bible. Their ministry has grown immensely and thrived since then. But here in May 2007, we discover they had just returned the night before from weeks of performing on the road. And they invite us to dine and stay as overnight guests! Hours earlier we were complete strangers.

The next morning, as we prepared to leave after a scrumptious breakfast, Cliff informs us that numerous tornadoes touched down yesterday and overnight in our planned direction of travel. In one community in southwest Kansas, a town with a population of three thousand, every home was destroyed. And now the weather pattern has stalled, dumping several inches of rain causing dangerous flooding.

Had we not accepted the invite and lingered to attend Cowboy Church, we most likely would have been in the thick of all that dangerous Midwest weather. Had we not accepted Cliff and Myra's invite to stay with them, who knows, but God, what danger lurked ahead for us.

Sometimes we have to let go of our plans. Sometimes we have to go with the flow spontaneously, so to speak. Sometimes it pays to trust others who may be intervening on our behalf. Sometimes we have to trust God to resolve a mystery. Thank you, Cliff and Myra, for being God's messengers. And we Praise God for His divine intervention. We also suggest you visit their website, http://biblealivetheater.com to learn more about their growing ministry.

How trusting are you? Are you still the captain of your soul? How's that working out for you?

One of the author's grandchildren was inspired to capture the image of the book's subtitle - "Bridging the chasm between God's will for our lives and ours".

# Divine Grace

The Greek word translated *charismata*, which conveys much more than its common English equivalent, spiritual gifts. The root, *charis*, means grace. The suffix, *mata*, means "portion of" or 'expression of'. In other words, what we have been calling a spiritual gift the scripture calls a concrete expression of grace.

—Jack Haberer in *The Contemporaries Met the Classics on The Holy Spirit*, Complied by Randall Harris, 2004 Howard Publishing

# Seeking Spiritual Growth

In his message on spiritual growth, a pastor once shared this to make his point: "How many Christians does it take to change a burned out light bulb?" Of course, the congregation stared silently waiting for the numerical punch line. "Change?" he asked, "Change?"

When we accept Christ as our personal savior, by faith in Him and by His grace we become transformed into the potential likeness of Jesus himself. No, not perfection, but by doing so, God fulfills His promise of placing His Holy Spirit within us. His presence is with us forever. The Holy Spirit becomes our guide and counsel, if we let him. This then allows us to grow and mature in our new relationship with God. This continuing process of maturity has a trigger—us. Too often we become complacent and satisfied with what is sometimes referred to as "doing church." But our Christian responsibility is to continually seek to grow both in knowledge and experience of God. In First Corinthians 11:1, the Apostle Paul says, "Follow my example, as I follow the example of Christ." To become more Christ like is up to us. The more we squeeze our trigger and desire to grow in our faith, the faster the process.

This growth process can be referred to as discipleship or sanctification. Theologians and Christian writers have authored many books on the subject and some of my favorites are listed in the Appendix. What is important to know, however, is that this desire to mature is primarily our decision. Once we have decided to accept Jesus, we can become, as one Christian author inferred, a fan or, preferably, a follower of Christ.

In this section of *A Call to Inspire,* we've included some personal experiences that highlighted the meaning of growing in our faith—honest spiritual transformation.

# Simple Question, Profound Answer

Defining moments are significant interruptions that so deeply influence our life that we experience a paradigm shift in our behavior. Our new behavior then leads to subsequent amazing events. Put another way, a defining moment is singularly the point at which the essential nature or character of a person is revealed.

Even nations can experience defining moments. America has had many in its history. President's Park in Washington, DC officially recognizes fourteen major events: the Revolutionary War and Independence, the Civil War and Reconstruction, and the terrorist attack of 9/11, to name a few.

For Jews and Christians, the Tanakh (or Miqra) and the Bible, respectively, are filled with many such defining moments in the history of God's people. All throughout scripture, one can read about the amazing events that followed such moments. The most well-known event involved Moses. He was a Jewish boy rescued from death by Egyptian royalty who, as an adult, murdered an Egyptian in a fit of rage, fled Egypt in fear of his life, and spent the next forty years as a simple shepherd. Perhaps he was less than ordinary? After his defining moment with God in the desert, Moses, though initially reluctant, obediently led God's chosen people out of slavery in Egypt to their Promised Land. It truly is a remarkable story of obedience, disobedience, miracles, and even God's wrath.

The defining moment for Moses was the burning bush; for Daniel, a lion's den; for the apostle Peter, walking on water; and for the Apostle Paul, the road to Damascus. You have likely experienced a defining moment. Once you did, you were not the same. For Linda and me, our defining moment was a question. Yes, a question.

94

Linda and I have shared how God worked supernaturally in our lives and the lives of those he divinely appointed to cross our paths many times. Often, some ask how or why do you think this happened to you. I usually say we believe in our case, it started with a defining moment in our spiritual life. In the mid-1990s, we were uprooted from our Connecticut home of twenty-eight years to San Diego. I was fifty-two, Linda forty-nine. A sudden business downsizing provided new opportunities within my employer United Technologies, Pratt & Whitney Division. The move found us in a new home and a new church family three thousand miles west. The new job assignment was officially temporary, meaning it would last three, perhaps four or five years, and I was given commensurate salary benefits—unusual for a domestic assignment.

This new job assignment was quite honestly not my preferred choice, but we gradually adjusted. Yet we wondered, *Was God at work?* We started calling our move to San Diego an adventure, primarily to appease ourselves. Three months into our adventure, Pastor Ken Licht of Tierrasanta Lutheran Church (now retired) required us to attend a new members' class. We balked strongly as we were cradle Christians and Lutherans and would not officially become members since my job assignment was temporary. We caved reluctantly. Pastor Ken began the class by asking the thirty-five of us to think about this question: "Where are you in your walk with God?"

*"Huh?"* My wife and I looked at each other quizzically. What is a walk with God? Well, Linda and I shared our past religious experience, but we were not convinced our answer was a walk with God. We had never been taught how to walk with God. If we were ever exposed to the idea, it never resonated with us. With Pastor Ken's help, we began to realize the answer was almost before our very eyes all along, but we had been blind to it. Since that moment in San Diego in October of 1996, Linda and I have been on a walk with God that differs significantly from our earlier behavior of regular church attendance and occasional Bible study and church fellowship.

Our new walk involved much more time with God in daily prayers, devotionals, Bible study more than once a week, and frequent fellowship with other believers. In short, more time spent with God and His Word. Doing so brings Him great joy because He loves us so unconditionally. When we do not communicate with Him often, He misses us. What a curious thought?

Call it an epiphany, defining or watershed moment, paradigm shift, or whatever. Our life has not been the same since hearing that question in the fall of 1996. In *A Call to Inspire,* Linda and I hope you're witnessing God's glory and his grace and perhaps a glimpse of an answer to the question: "Where are you in your walk with God?"

# Leaps of Faith

As long as I can remember, I always wanted to be a nurse. In high school, I belonged to the future nurse's society and became a "Volunteer" at our local hospital, the ones in the candy stripe uniform who did volunteer work. We performed several odd jobs including bringing mail and the gift cart to patient's rooms, plus getting fresh water for patients.

After graduating from Sharon General Hospital's three-year RN diploma program, I continued to work there for five months until marrying my sweetheart, Ken. We moved to Connecticut where I continued my nursing career at Manchester Hospital for another two and a half years. Three children were born over the next six years and they were my full-time job. During this time, I did manage to work a few hours at a local convalescent home in the evenings when Daddy got home from work.

After almost nine years of being away from hospital nursing, Ken discovered a re-entry to nursing program being offered at Hartford Hospital. Although it was just twenty minutes away, it meant driving in to the city. My desire to regain my skills overtook my fear of driving on the highway and going to a big city hospital. I took this leap of faith somewhat reluctantly, but I must say that I felt proud to be able to maneuver my way through the city streets and then find my way around the hospital. Following the re-entry program, I was hired by the hospital and continued to work there every other weekend for three years. I was a nurse once again and loved it.

After leaving Hartford Hospital, I returned to our local Manchester Hospital on a part time basis. Soon after that, Carla, a nurse friend I knew at our church asked me if I'd be interested in job sharing a private duty assignment with her. I declined, saying that I was happy with my job at the hospital. Over the next several years, Carla would periodically question me, "Linda, can I interest you in the job-sharing assignment with me?" My answer was always no. I had never done private duty nursing. It didn't really appeal to me.

Then one time she told me how her private duty assignment with Ashlee was taking a new path. Ashlee, who had been born with SMA or spinal muscular atrophy and was paralyzed from the nose down, was starting a preschool program. Carla said she really needed someone to split the week of taking her to school. After a day or so of praying about her request, I decided to take another leap of faith. I said yes and went through the process of being hired by the agency overseeing Ashlee's care. Carla also took me to meet Ashlee and her mother.

The first thing I noticed when I entered Ashlee's room was this tiny child with beautiful curly brown hair on a big hospital bed with lots of noisy equipment around her. She was paralyzed from the nose down and her mouth was constantly open in the oval shape of an O. Ashlee had a tracheotomy and could not breathe on her own, so there was a ventilator that did her breathing for her. Because of the trach, she also needed frequent suctioning. A bag hanging from an IV pole held the feeding tube that entered her abdomen through a G-tube.

I knew about her condition but wasn't prepared for what I saw. And I must admit I was a little intimidated at first, and rightly so. Reflecting back on the nine years that I cared for Ashlee, there never was just a routine day. You always had to be prepared for the unexpected.

When I first started working with Ashlee, she communicated via a communication board. With a slight pressure in the palm of one hand to operate the board, Ashlee was able to point to different pictures. During my time with Ashlee, her communication eventually evolved into a very sophisticated, digitized speech machine, called a light talker and later, another device called a liberator.

This talking device with the liberator consisted of rows of icons. Their location would be identified by letters and numbers depending on where they were on the board. One icon might just be a word while another could be a sentence. For example, 4A might represent "goodbye" and 7B might represent "I need to go to bed." Ashlee was able to operate a switch that controlled a light that scanned the board by using a tiny muscle located on her palm between her thumb and forefinger. Operating the computerized voice was one thing, but she also learned to program it and had to memorize where everything was located on the board. And Ashlee was teaching us in the process.

And as she got older, Ashlee's vocabulary grew and the conversation combinations on the board became more complex. Now it took two icon combinations to say something. For example, 1A and 3A might say, "I need to go to the bathroom," while 1A and 6F would say, "What is your name?" Ashlee also would blink her beautiful brown eyes for yes and give you a penetrating stare for no answers. Just being with her, I discovered that Ashlee was also teaching me how to understand her nonverbal communications.

Ashlee was the first severely handicapped child mainstreamed into the classroom at Lakeview Elementary School in Vernon, Connecticut. Before her arrival, a special assembly was held to inform the students and teachers about her condition. This did not relieve her first-grade teacher's fear of having another adult (Carla and me) in her classroom and such a needy child. Carla and I tried to be as unobtrusive as possible when we cared for Ashlee. But there was no denying that the suction machine made noise. And seeing Ashlee in her wheelchair and accompanying equipment was a distraction for the kids. It didn't take long for the children to become accustomed to Ashlee and her nurses. It was a treat for them to be able to help push her wheel chair or to be her helper.

Ashlee had the patience of a saint. Think for a moment about being totally dependent. She could do nothing for herself. And using her liberator took time. For her to say something might take several minutes. Ashlee was teaching me patience. I had to wait sometimes minutes for her to communicate.

One particular sad incident I remember was during summer school. Her new teacher decided it was important for Ashlee to say good morning to her when we arrived in the classroom. For whatever reason, Ashlee decided not to say the greeting. The teacher tried disciplining her by taking away privileges, such as art time, which Ashlee loved. When that didn't work, she sent home instructions that Ashlee was not to watch TV. Ashlee still would not greet this teacher, although it would've been very easy for her to do it. Ashlee never did say good morning to this teacher. Carla and I admired Ashlee's stubbornness. The teacher's negative behavior modification technique did not produce her desired results. Here, this little girl had no control of anything except her speech, and this teacher tried to take even that away.

In many ways, Ashlee was like other children her age. She loved hair ribbons, having her nails painted, and the Muppets of television fame. It became evident that Ashlee was very artistic and creative. She couldn't do anything physically but would have her own ideas on colors and placement of things. As she got older, she also loved trips to the mall, scrapbooking, and crafts. Another passion was watching NASCAR races on TV.

Over the years, Carla and I noticed certain students gravitated toward Ashlee. Sara and Cathy were two that not only helped Ashlee in school but would come to her house to visit with her. And Sara once mentioned that she wanted to work in medicine and work with handicapped people like Ashlee.

Ashlee far exceeded her life expectancy by twenty-seven years. Although she was paralyzed and spent her life in a wheelchair, she was not speechless. In fact, her persistence, patience, stubbornness, and communication, many times left us speechless. Ashlee touched so many lives—fellow students, teachers, medical staff, her parents, siblings and especially me—all without physically touching them or me. I believe she taught us more than we taught her.

I intended to have a normal nursing career working in the hospital. But God intended that I take continuing leaps of faith so that I could spend nine years with a paralyzed child who was unable to speak yet could teach me lessons in life like no one else could. I also learned through those leaps of faith that God's ways are better, far better, than our ways.

Is your walk with God based on faith or something else? When fear, worry or anxiety encroach, on whom or what do you place your trust? It takes humility, not pride, to trust God. Only then can we surrender to the one who truly cares for us (1 Peter 5:6–7).

# Withering Heights

Sometimes facing a fear requires supernatural help. My fear is alto-phobia or fear of heights. I've had this fear as long as I can remember. Altophobia has caused me to miss some great views and vistas that one finds at such places as the Grand Canyon or Bryce Canyon. Let me take you on a hike in Bryce Canyon with Ken and me.

"This begins the next leg of our 2007 southwest Awedyssee." That was my journal entry on Saturday, March 10, 2007, as we left Cumming, Georgia, on that cool fifty two-degree rainy morning. We had left our home in Connecticut on February 27 on our long awaited and planned cross-country retirement trip. Good bye to the freezing temps and five inches of snow on the ground. The last ten days had been spent visiting our two daughters and their families in Cumming.

Ken had retired two years before me and had been researching and planning our route and itinerary during that time—just a direction and definitely no interstates. We were taking the byways and heading to the southwest.

Oh, the stories I could tell you of our travels thru Alabama, Texas, New Mexico, Arizona, and California. But this story actually begins in Utah nine years earlier in June of 1998. We were living in San Diego at the time and decided to take an extended weekend trip to some of the national parks, including Bryce Canyon.

We were enjoying a breakfast pastry in a little coffee shop in Bryce Canyon National Park after stopping at Sunrise Point to take in the early morning view. Ken had wanted to take a trail that led down in to the canyon with steep drop offs, but because of my fear of heights, I was unable to go. Sweet husband that he is, he decided to give up the walk and stay with me. For the next half hour, he prayed for me and with me.

An hour later, success and prayers answered, we did go a short distance on that trail, enough to give us a taste of Bryce Canyon. It was a taste that made us long for more. The beauty of Bryce Canyon is unique.

So fast forwarding to Thursday April 19, 2007, we are at the Bryce Canyon visitor's center talking to one of the park rangers about day-hike trail options. Ken had already looked at a map and mentioned the Fairyland Trail, to which the ranger exclaimed, "My favorite trail in the park." He said it was about a four- to five-hour hike or longer depending on your pace and how many times you stop to take photographs. He assured me that I didn't have to worry about edges which are one of my big fears that go along with heights.

We took his advice on where to park and started off toward what we thought was the trailhead. Another family was beginning their hike and informed us we needed to go the opposite direction to get to Sunrise Point where the trail began. They contradicted the park ranger, but let's hike with some companions. So off we went with camera, binoculars, and a packed lunch and water for a day-hike. The air was chilly at forty-seven degrees, but there was no wind and we were comfortably dressed. The trail followed along the upper canyon rim for about two miles, and yes, I could stay away from that edge. Then we reached Sunrise Point where the Fairyland Trail descended gradually into the canyon a few thousand feet. Here we bid farewell to our companions. But here I was now following the same trail down into the canyon I feared so much just seven years earlier. No problem this time.

After we had gone way beyond where we had previously traveled, I looked back at Ken and smiled and said, "What do you think? Am I doing good?" He replied that he hadn't wanted to say anything for fear of making me aware of what I was accomplishing!

It was awesome! And I was excited to be doing it and overcoming my prior fear of edges and heights. The trail led us up and down several canyons. Just when you thought you were coming to the end, you would have another canyon to cross. Every bend in the trail brought another Kodak moment for Ken. We were blessed with a beautiful day, bright blue skies and no clouds. The scenery was breathtaking. Ken was snapping photos frequently.

It was a fun hike until we came to my biggest challenge—a knife edge. That's where our path was about thirty-five feet long and a narrow two feet across and where the sides sloped down hundreds of feet on either side without any shrubs or trees, just a barren slope. Yikes! By this time, we had been hiking six hours and it was already late afternoon and it was not an option to turn back.

Trust me. I didn't want to do it but knew I didn't have a choice. After prayers and many false starts and cajoling by Ken, I inched my way across the knife edge. I think I collapsed with relief once I reached the far side. I also remember saying to Ken that it was good that I didn't know about it when we started our hike.

Little did I know that ahead of me was my worst nightmare. It was about another half hour of walking when we knew we were getting close to the end of the trail and the end of daylight. The trail appeared to wind along a cliff wall. "No, that can't be our trail," Ken said. And I quickly agreed with him. But it actually was the trail. We could actually see the end abut one hundred yards ahead.

As we approached where the trail began its narrow snake-like path, I glanced at the deep drop-off and immediately collapsed in tears, paralyzed in fear. I cried, "I can't do this." For the next ten to twenty minutes, I cried and then tried to think of alternatives. No chance to turn back. It was definitely too late in the day and that frightening knife edge was behind me. Another thought I had was for Ken to go ahead and get help and perhaps have them helicopter me out of my predicament. While I was lamenting, Ken tried to find an alternate way up the cliff wall. None was found due the steepness of the slope.

It was during this time that I began praying and remembered an earlier devotion we had read that morning. The scripture was the Twenty-Third Psalm. Okay, I had halfway composed myself and reconciled that I had no choice but to walk this very narrow, barely-a-foot-wide trail. Ken coached me to keep my left hand up shielding my view of the deep drop-off on my left that was hundreds of feet below. On my right was the steep canyon wall. I insisted he walk ahead of me and I inched my way along saying, "The Lord is my Shepherd . . . The Lord is my Shepherd . . ." repeatedly. Every five minutes or so, I would put the Twenty-Third Psalm on hold and ask Ken if he could see the end of the trail.

"No," he replied, "but you're doing great. Keep it up." Finally, after what seemed like an eternity, we did reach the end and I did collapse in tears of relief. I still can't believe I did it.

There was our car just a short distance away. That is when we realized that if we had gone in the direction we had started out before that family informed us to go the opposite direction, we would have seen how treacherous that part of the trail was and we never would have attempted the complete trail loop!

If there ever was a divine aspect, it was the morning devotion on the Twenty-Third Psalm. Ken and I intended to have a close encounter with Bryce Canyon by day-hiking a trail. God intended to teach me how grow in my faith and to overcome a paralyzing fear by trusting Him. This was a classic example, though thankfully brief, of how my faith—our faith—can get us through trials until we get to the other side.

Our Lord is not only a good Shepherd; He's also a good teacher. Well, I never could have walked the narrow precipice without Him, that's for sure! Who do trust when you encounter unexpected trials or trails?

# Uplifting Grace

And He who searches our hearts knows the mind
of the Spirit, because the Spirit intercedes for God's
people in accordance with the Will of God
—Romans 8:27

In July of 1995, my wife had a serious life-threatening fall from her bike while we were vacationing in Upstate New York. Linda's traumatic brain injury had our family and friends, and especially me, seriously concerned. There were too many unknowns.

After notifying our pastor, Paul Henry, in Connecticut, he immediately contacted a pastor in Watertown, New York, where Linda was hospitalized in a coma in ICU. Every day for the next week, Pastor Paul Luisi visited Linda's bedside. I was so grateful for his presence and calming influence during a very trying time and uncertain future. Linda awakened from the coma after five days, and very gradually healed over the next five years. Praise God!

Now fast forward to July 2011. We had a cash offer on our Connecticut home with a closing on July 25. Our plans were to place the belongings we did not donate or sell into storage, travel the USA for three months, and then look for a new home somewhere in north Georgia near our two daughter's families. Georgia, or most places in the southeast, were far more retirement-friendly, financially speaking, than Connecticut.

In cleaning out my desk, I came across Pastor Luisi's business card, which included his email address, and decided that I was long overdue in giving him an update on Linda's medical status. Little did I know that his reply would be a such an uplifting surprise.

Dear Ken and Linda, What a delight hearing from you! I remember both of you well and give thanks to God for Linda's recovery. She certainly has been blessed having you at her side. It's amazing you contacted me when you did. The other day I again watched the wonderful film *Big Fish*. Have you seen it? If not, I highly recommend it. As the lead character faces death and reflects on his life, people whom he helped along the way are introduced to the viewer. Mary, my wife, asked me how many people I thought whom I had helped throughout the years either as a physician's assistant or as a pastor ever thinks of me. Lo, and behold, your email arrived! I will print it and keep it always. All of us need to be validated from time to time and your email has done just that.

Sixteen years had elapsed before I thought to give Pastor Paul Luisi, who so graciously visited us, the courtesy of a simple update and thank you. But that elapsed time was according to God's will. I intended to provide an update on Linda's recovery, but God intended my email to provide an emotional uplift to someone who had done so much for so many during his two careers—at just the right time!

Are you overdue in giving someone a special thank you? If so, perhaps your message may be timed perfectly according to God's will.

# Pistachio Rocks

*May 4, 2017, Chiricahua National Monument, Arizona*

While driving east on Interstate 10 in southeast Arizona, a billboard advertising pistachio nuts not only caught my eye but also captured my curiosity. Arizona pistachios? Ten years ago, this part of Arizona was uninhabited desert. Now we see fields of irrigated trees and vineyards. Some enlightened visionaries made it happen. At the next exit we found the shop advertised on the billboard, tasted many varieties of pistachios and pecans, and made a few delicious purchases. Then Linda made a curious discovery.

A brochure at the checkout showed a photo of what looked like the hoodoos in Bryce Canyon, but these were green and gray, not orange and yellow. Upon questioning, we were told that the Chiricahua National Monument or Wonderland of Rocks was just a short thirty-five mile drive south. It was once the hideout of Geronimo and his Apache tribe. Intrigued, we postponed our planned bike ride in White Sands, New Mexico and headed south. Our given shortcut was about twenty miles on a dirt road, part of once-famous southwest wagon trail that went past Fort Bowie.

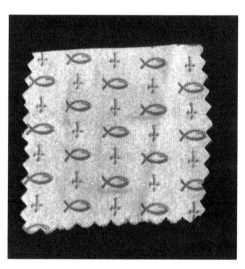

Upon arriving at our destination, a ranger directed us to the best scenic trail—three miles long and several hundred feet of elevation change—in the Rocks and suggested a clockwise direction to minimize knee pain on the step type terrain. At the trailhead, we encountered a young woman and her husband who said they were visiting from Germany and just finished their hike. When I inquired about their direction, she insisted that a counterclockwise direction was best, with a gradual ascent finish, confiding that her husband had two knee replacements and did just fine. So we altered our plans for a second time today, or did *we?* We also gave the woman a couple of pocket crosses, a small foam cross sewn in a square piece of Christian fish symbol fabric, when she began sharing about a friend with terminal cancer. Thank you, Lord.

Halfway into our hike amidst these giant hoodoo rock formations, we met a couple coming the opposite direction. Unlike two ships passing in the night, our brief chat lingered for almost an hour. Janette and church organist husband Sandy were from Scotland of all places. Both are devout believers and members of a Presbyterian church! We had much to talk about and share. Time was forgotten. What a delightful interesting couple who, like us, love to travel. Curiously, we met no one else during our four-hour hike!

We captured numerous digital images of the unusual scenery, but the image that remains most indelibly is the selfie we took of us—a nation and an ocean apart but together in spirit and a moment in time. Our friendship continues to this day via frequent email.

A highway billboard led to a newly grown pistachio orchard, which led to an unplanned journey in a wonderland of rocks with an amazing experience of divine grace, showing how God can even use inanimate objects like a sign, a nut, and a rock to produce His fruit of the spirit—"love, joy, peace, kindness, goodness" (Galatians 5:23), and everlasting friendship.

Is your spontaneity serendipitous? Don't let your plans miss divine opportunities.

Authors with Janette and Sandy McLuckie,
visiting United States from Scotland

Hunter Nurmi Age 8

One of the author's grandchildren was inspired to capture the image of the book's subtitle - "Bridging the chasm between God's will for our lives and ours".

# *Divine Reminders*

The most beautiful experience we can have is the mysterious. It is the fundamental emotion that stands at the cradle of true art and true science. Whoever does not know it and can no longer wonder, no longer marvel, is as good as dead, and his eyes are dimmed.

—Albert Einstein

# Convincing Winks

Have you ever looked at another person, perhaps a relative, close friend, or even a loved one and received a smile and a wink from them? Such simple expressions of love can give you a warm fuzzy feeling, one of true joy. It's brief, silent, yet very convincing.

During our travels and sometimes just going to and fro near our home, we have had many such brief yet convincing "winks" from God. Some folks call them God-winks, others God-incidences, but whatever you name them, they are reassuring faith-building reminders that He is in our midst.

## Perfect Gift

While traveling in the Midwest during the spring of 2007, we had an unplanned visit with a friend. A spontaneous thought of her led to an evening invite for dinner. Later, as we were about to depart, she insisted so strongly that we stay overnight with her that we ditched our normal motel plans. In doing so, we learned, sadly, that her husband of more than thirty years had left her that very day. We prayed long and hard with her before retiring. The next morning, we were led to give her a small token of our appreciation, a recently purchased book that we believed would help someone emotionally distressed. Linda had purchased the book at a women's retreat a few weeks earlier. Two weeks later, our distraught friend emailed us saying that she believed we were sent by God at the right time and the gift of the book was perfect. She even bought more copies for friends. Very spontaneously, we intended to visit a long-time friend we hadn't seen in years; God intended it to be an unexpected but needed blessing for someone severely hurting emotionally.

## Surprise Anniversary Toast

At a Best Western in Van Horn, Texas, we pulled into a parking space at dusk. Inside, while waiting to check-in, another senior couple approached us saying, "We noticed your license plate from Connecticut. We're from back east too."

We were strangers who then spent the next three hours, including sharing fellowship over dinner, together. This couple lived in central Pennsylvania, our home state in an area very familiar to us. One of the many special things about this couple is that they began their journey spending a week in Louisiana helping residents there to rebuild after a devastating hurricane. Now they were on a retirement journey like ours, long on itinerary but short on schedule. We felt so blessed that they spoke up and agreed to share time with us. The following week, they would celebrate forty-nine years of marriage—a special blessing. We intended to just check-in to our motel and grab a meal alone someplace. God intended us to meet another Christian couple, share time over dinner together, treat them to a Happy Anniversary toast, and part ways feeling better than when we arrived.

## Spiritual Medicine

Monday, April 23, 2007, Moab, Utah. Where are you in your walk with God? Do you feel close or distant? Who do you think moved? I believe these are questions that all of us should ask ourselves from time to time. It's good spiritual medicine. During our travels, in fact, through much of our 7,800 miles to date, Beeba (Linda's grandma name) and I have had little surprising messages that lead us to believe that God is with us on our Awedyssee in between the times He randomly uses us in supernatural ways in divine encounters with strangers.

Every morning during our travels, with few exceptions, Beeba and I begin our day with a Bible devotion from one of three devotional booklets. Today, we drove to a remote area outside of Moab, to one of the Petro glyph (Native American writing) sites. We randomly chose one of the three devotional books. The Bible reading for today's devotion was from the Book of Ruth. As we read the assigned Bible verses, they identified Ruth and her mother-in-law, Naomi, as women from Moab.

Naturally, Beeba and I stopped reading for a moment, paused for a short prayer, and thanked the Lord for reminding us of his closeness. In our travels without a schedule and so many other places we could be on the map today, we chose to be in Moab, Utah! And from three devotional books, we chose the one that mentioned the Biblical Moab, or did we? Was it coincidence or the universe in divine harmony? You decide.

## Surrender

Growing up in a traditional church has a special meaning to me (Ken). I developed a special interest in the hymns we sang, especially the older ones. As a history buff, I was curious about the writer and his/her inspiration. Luther's *A Mighty Fortress*, Newton's *Amazing Grace*, and Boberg's *How Great Thou Art* are a few of those classics with an enduring appeal. They focus on the glory and grandeur of God.

One classic, *I Surrender All*, had and still has a bittersweet impact on me to this day. As much as I love the words and their meaning, I have trouble feeling capable of surrendering all. When I sing the hymn, I can't but feel a bit hypocritical. When I searched its history, I made a couple of interesting discoveries. A book titled *Hymn Stories* revealed that the writer of *I Surrender All*, Judson W. Van Deventer (1855–1939), studied Art in the late 1800s. He became not only a teacher, but as public schools were being established, Judson became the Supervisor of Art for the public school system in, of all places, my hometown of Sharon, Pennsylvania. That surely hit home and puzzled me even more. While in Sharon, which borders Ohio, Judson traveled to Ohio frequently to listen to evangelists.

He later wrote: "At last the pivotal hour of my life came and I surrendered all. A new day was ushered into my life. I became an evangelist and discovered deep down in my soul a talent hitherto unknown to me. God had hidden a song in my heart, and touching a tender chord, caused me to sing a song I had never sung before." Judson wrote many hymns during his evangelistic ministry, but *I Surrender All* is his most famous.

In his later years, Judson retired in Florida. Many people, pastors, and friends who had heard him preach came to visit and thank him for touching their lives. One of those who visited just passed away recently, the greatest evangelist of our time—Billy Graham (1918–2018).

I intended to research a hymn that simultaneously both touches my heart and disturbs me. God intended, I believe, to provide some insight about a hymn that can lead me to my future home but also a hymn that surprisingly led me to my hometown.

## *Favorite Saying*

Friends Linda and Dan live in the beautiful Pocono Mountains of Northeastern Pennsylvania. We came to know this delightful couple after many years of visiting their small business in the area. During one of our travels north from Georgia to visit with our son's family in Connecticut, they invited us to spend a weekend with them. During our stay, I noticed Dan's passionate interest in a particular subject. Photos and signs of his passion decorated the walls of his den. A week later, during our family visit, we made a day-trip to Watch Hill, Rhode Island, where hot lobster rolls from the Bay Street Deli are a tasty bonus. While browsing the various shops that day, I noticed a hand-painted sign that would be uniquely appropriate for Dan's den, one I did not see on his wall. We quickly made a purchase and decided, rather than mail it, to drop it off by taking a route passed their Pennsylvania home on our way south.

We contacted Linda and Dan and arranged for a brief stop. After presenting the gifted sign to Dan, he was ecstatically surprised. He quickly fetched a photo of himself many years ago in his former office at work. The same hand-painted sign we had just given him was hanging behind him. It was a favorite saying of his but his office sign somehow disappeared over the years. Sometimes our Lord blesses us with special pleasant surprises. How well do you listen and respond to that still small voice, that hunch, that speaks to you?

## A Five Dollar Bill

Does God really pay attention to minor details, even honest mistakes in our life? Chris DiCio, a neighbor and close friend, had a temporary physical ailment that prevented her from driving. She called and asked my wife to take her to a doctor's appointment. The doctor's office was in mid-town Atlanta where they had to pay $5 to park upon entry to the parking garage. As they walked from the parking garage, they discovered that they inadvertently parked in the wrong garage and the doctor's office, though close by, was too far to walk. They returned to the car a bit upset they paid five bucks for nothing but a mistake.

After paying another five dollars upon entry to the correct garage, they inquired at the doctor's office for a parking voucher. "Sorry, no vouchers," the receptionist said. "Oh, well, that's really ten dollars," Chris thought. Following the doctor's visit, Linda drove Chris to a restaurant near our home. After exiting and locking the car, something blew by on the ground and landed at Chris's feet. It was a five-dollar bill! "Can you believe this?" Chris said excitedly as she picked it up and showed Linda. Angered earlier by a mistaken garage fee, they were more than pleasantly surprised by the return of the exact amount of a mistaken payment. They crossed the parking lot and entered the restaurant praising God, for He had directed them to a specific place at a specific time. God cares, even in the small things.

## *Look at Us*

While living on a small lake in Connecticut some years ago, we enjoyed sharing our waterfront lifestyle. We very often used our pontoon boat to cruise around with friends and neighbors— breakfast, lunch, dinner and even moonlight cruises. We decided to treat one of our neighbors, Jean and Fran, to a special treat, an anniversary cruise. They had a few years on us, were still active, but lacked any of the water craft. Fran turned his retirement lifestyle into award-winning stained glass window, lampshade, and even old building replica hobby. Jean loved to write and also won awards for her short stories.

I had been playing guitar for a few years, so I decided to play and sing while we were anchored far out from shore and shared some cake my wife Linda had made. I started to play and sing "Look at Us," a love song made famous by country singer Vince Gill. I was only into the first refrain when I noticed tears rolling down Jean's cheeks and noticed Fran's eyes getting watery. After I finished, I jokingly said, "I didn't realize my singing was that bad that it would bring you to tears."

Jean looked up at me and said, still teary, "How did you know that song was our favorite and has been for many years?" I told them I had no idea, but I was glad that I chose it for you. "I just thought it would be appropriate," I added.

We had intended to treat a neighbor to a short anniversary cruise. God intended to use me supernaturally to provide an emotional uplift to a special couple. God enjoys reminding us of His love.

Chloe Nurmi  Age 5

One of the author's grandchildren was inspired to
capture the image of the book's subtitle - "Bridging the
chasm between God's will for our lives and ours".

# Divine Providence
## Attempt Something So Great

Attempt something so great for God that
it is doomed to failure, lest He be in it.
—Dr. John Edmond Haggai,
Founder, Haggai International

William Carey (1761–1834) became a Calvinist Baptist preacher but only after seeing himself as morally bankrupt and in need of a crucified Savior for pardon and salvation. He possessed a keen intellect and taught himself dozens of languages and dialects. He developed a passion for missions telling his comrades, "Expect great things from God; attempt great things for God." Reluctantly, due to Carey's dogged persistence, the Baptist Association agreed to form what eventually became the Baptist Missionary Society. Carey went to India in 1793 and ministered there until his death. "His comprehensive missional approach led to establishing schools, hospitals, a savings bank, a Bengali newspaper, teaching languages at a local college, founding the first Christian college in India" and much more, in addition to evangelization. "He expected great things from God, and attempted great things for God, and God brought them to pass. Contemporary ministers called him the 'hair-brained enthusiast', but we know him as the father of modern missions. (From *the One Year Christian History,* by E. Michael and Sharon Rusten, Tyndale House 2003).

# Attempt Something So Great

## *How Did All This Happen?*

Having read the preceding chapters, you are either amazed, puzzled, or both. Those two reactions are exactly what Linda and I could read on the faces in the groups who listened to us sharing our experiences. Some listeners, sadly, gave an impression that they felt incapable of having such experiences even though we emphasized that the power of the Holy Spirit resides in all believers. Others were intrigued and curious to know how it happened.

The reaction I recall most was after our first prepared talk at a church in Aiken, South Carolina, in January 2008. A less-than-middle-age man asked, "How did all this happen? What did you do to experience all those amazing events, because I want that to happen in my life every day?"

His encouraging question caught us by surprise. Our experiences, especially the variety and magnitude of them, were new to us and we didn't fully understand them. So I answered by saying, "I wish I had a truly knowledgeable answer for you. Neither Linda nor I are seminary graduates. We were taught from the pulpit, Sunday school, and Bible studies on the Father, Son, and Holy Scriptures. So I need to do more study on the Holy Spirit myself. But this much I can tell you. Before leaving on our journey last spring, Linda and I prayed daily for over two months, asking the Lord to use us as His instruments during our travels. We believe we were led to intentionally not schedule a detailed itinerary, hoping to be on God's time more than ours. And then we trusted God to use us and were open to His guidance, especially interruptions in our plans. We were even prepared to serve Him our way—entertaining at nursing homes, but we never entered even one. Yet, almost daily, we had these divine appointments. So what I can tell you now is that prayer, being on God's time, and trust and obedience to His promptings are very important keys."

At the guiding of the Holy Spirit, we were invited to give many other talks to church groups over the next few years. Audience responses were similar. During that time, I studied what the Bible had to say and accumulated a small library of books on the Holy Spirit. I discovered that my answer to that first question we received was pretty accurate. Some of those books are listed at the end of this chapter.

## *God's Role*

In the introduction to *A Call to Inspire* we posed a few important questions, questions about God's will for our lives—How can we be sure it is happening without any doubt? And does it happen without our cooperation with God?

There are many Bible passages that tell us about God's plan for our lives. First and foremost of these are: (1) He has a unique plan for every believer according to Jeremiah 29:11: "For I know the plans I have for you," declares the Lord, "plans to prosper you and not to harm you, plans to give you hope and a future;" (2) Proverbs 3:5–6 provides some specific insight: "Trust in the Lord with all your heart and lean not on your own understanding; in all your ways submit to Him, and He will make your paths straight;" and (3) Hebrews 10:36 indicates a reward for our trust and perseverance: "You need to persevere so that when you have done the will of God, you will receive what He has promised." You'll note that scripture does not provide a specific blueprint. God's will for our lives is uniquely individual.

*"For, my thoughts are not your thoughts, neither are your ways my ways, declares the Lord"* (Isaiah 55:8). Using this and other similar Bible verses, Christians are led to believe that God cares for and directs all things with His wisdom and love. His sovereignty is referred to

as the doctrine of divine providence. I will leave the in-depth study of God's divine providence and our free-will for the reader's choice, but it is important for you to be aware that the authors believe divine providence is an integral part of our life experiences, including those we shared in *A Call to Inspire*. The Merriam-Webster Dictionary definition of divine providence is: (a) divine guidance or care and (b) God conceived as the power sustaining and guiding human destiny. For example, two or more individuals can act in the same event and produce a given outcome without both individuals having the same intent.

## Providence and Free Will

For example, in April of 1994, my wife and I were awakened from our sleep by a call from Linda's father. Her mom had died of a heart attack at age seventy-two while being treated for pneumonia in the hospital. We packed suitcases and the car quickly as we could and within a few hours we were heading west from Connecticut to Pennsylvania on Interstate 84. About an hour and a half into our drive, we pulled into a rest stop in New York State. I pulled up next to the only car, an early vintage classic Mustang. After using the rest room, I was the first one back to the car. A man was sitting on a picnic table smoking a cigarette in front of the Mustang. We struck up a conversation about his car and he said he was driving to Carlisle, Pennsylvania, for the annual classic car show. Then, abruptly changing the subject, he asked, "What's the longest bridge?" I was caught by surprise by the question but began tossing out some names of famous bridges across the United States. He nodded his head negative and, smiling, handed me a small pamphlet. By this time, the rest of the family was in the car and we bid each other farewell and safe travels.

Six hours later, we arrived at our destination. Linda's dad greeted us emotionally at the door. We hugged for a long time and then he said to me, "Kenny, I want you to talk about Garnet at the funeral service." He knew I was a lay pastor, but I'd never delivered a eulogy before and began praying for the right words. I remembered the pamphlet the classic Mustang guy had given me and began reading it. It was titled "What Is the Longest Bridge?" The content was all about Jesus. Jesus is the bridge between earth and heaven! Days later, at the service in church, I spoke about Linda's mom as the family knew her; how she became known affectionately as *Mugga*—a term of endearment given to her by our son, her first grandchild; and then I spoke at length after asking the question "What is the longest bridge?"

"What comes to mind? The Golden Gate in San Francisco or the George Washington in New York City? That's what came to my mind." I repeated the question three times and then asked, "Isn't that question one that we should all be asking ourselves? Do we know Jesus as our bridge to eternity?"

After the service, many commented about the message, but one in particular really moved me to tears. My Aunt Phyllis said this to me in private about her husband: "I've never seen your uncle cry before. But when you began talking about the longest bridge, he had tears rolling down his cheeks."

Earlier that week, I had, unknowingly, a divine encounter. A complete stranger intended to share an evangelistic message with me at an Interstate rest stop. God intended our meeting and that message to be appropriately shared at a funeral service for my mother-in-law, prompt listeners to think about their eternity, and move at least one listener, if not more, to emotional tears.

*"A man's heart plans his way; but the Lord directs his steps"* (Proverbs 16:9, NKJV).

## Historical Examples

Some Biblical examples of divine providence include Genesis Chapters 37–50—the story of Joseph; the Book of Job—how God permitted evil (Satan) to accomplish His will for Job; and perhaps the best example is the death of Christ, where God ordained Christ's crucifixion by evil men to bring about Christ's resurrection and the good intention of salvation to those who believe in Jesus as their

Savior. While evil is not an attribute of God, He can use it to fulfill His will for mankind.

*"As for you, you meant it for evil against me, but God meant it for good, to bring it about that many people should be kept alive, as they are today"* (Joseph to his brothers, Genesis 50:20, ESV).

All throughout history God has used individuals to serve His specific purpose. In their unique devotional, *The One Year Christian History* (Tyndale 2003), authors E. Michael and Sharon Rusten include these examples:

In 1738, George Whitefield, an Oxford graduate, left England for America. His ship anchored off Gibraltar for two weeks for unknown reasons. Whitefield, a new convert to Christianity, went ashore and for the two weeks the ship was anchored, he ministered to over a hundred British soldiers. How do you view interruptions to your schedule?

In 1856, an Irish woman in Ulster spoke her mind unexpectedly during an afternoon tea on a subject dear to her heart—the condition of our souls. From that one conversation, some attendees were moved to discuss the subject further. Conversations multiplied until they led to the Great Ulster Revival in 1859. Do you have such conviction?

In the late 1880s, some Cambridge students who were popular and athletically gifted, became friends. Known as The Cambridge Seven, they all became missionaries to China in 1885. Their popularity inspired many others: nearly eight hundred missionaries by 1900. Are you willing to be transformed for God's use?

## Our Role

So, if God has a plan, what is our role? In the introduction we asked: Why does there seem to be such a great chasm between God's will for our lives and our burning desire to see His will happen in us? The Bible says that the great chasm that separates us from God is sin or our willful disobedience of God's law. Due to God's grace, an attribute of God that is described as favor toward the unworthy, the bridge over that chasm is God's Son, Jesus. It is important that we have a personal relationship with Jesus just as Jesus had with His disciples. In his first letter to Timothy, the Apostle Paul says, *"For this is good and acceptable in the sight of God our Savior, who desires all men to be saved and to come to the knowledge of the truth"* (1 Timothy 2: 3–4, ESV). Another disciple, Luke, infers that Jesus wants us to become true followers, not just fans— *"Then He said to them all, 'If anyone desires to come after Me, let him deny himself, and take up his cross daily, and follow Me'."* (Luke 9:23). And lastly, James, another disciple, says that Jesus promises to give us insight, or wisdom, if we ask in prayer— *"If any of you lacks wisdom, let him ask of God, who gives all liberally and without reproach, and it will be given to him"* (James 1:5).

Throughout this book, we've used the words *we let* the Holy Spirit use us. Those words were given to us by a wise Pastor, Jeff Harter, to remind us of our personal role in being used by the Spirit. The apostle John spoke in John 7:37–39, of God's promise: *"He who believes in me, as the Scripture has said, out of his heart will flow rivers of living water."*

Think of the Holy Spirit this way: The Holy Spirit in us is like priming of the pump in the well. To get the living water flowing out of us to serve God's will for our life, we must do our part—pump the handle. In the devotional *One Year at His Feet* (Tyndale 2003), author Chris Tiegreen reminds us that "God brought the Israelites through the Red Sea, but only after Moses lifted up the staff. God brought down the walls of Jericho, but only after Joshua led the people through the right steps. God conquered Goliath, but only after David stepped onto the battlefield. And Jesus kept Peter afloat, but only after Peter got out of the boat." Are you—we—confidently ready to lift, lead, step or get out of our comfort zone?

Doing so, the authors believe, will enable you to develop a personal relationship with the resurrected Jesus; lead you to grow in faith; provide needed sustenance to get through trials in this life; and prompt a life of service for God's glory—all that by being led by the Spirit.

Perhaps an analogy by Oscar Hammerstein may help explain. Shortly before his death, Hammerstein penned the following:

A bell is no bell till you ring it
A song is no song till you sing it
Love in your heart wasn't put there to stay
Love isn't love till you give it away

Whether it's a bell, a song, or love, it requires action on our part to fulfill its purpose. Likewise, for God to fulfill His purpose in us, we must be confidently willing to do our part.

## Spontaneous Prayer

One action on our part, we discovered, was praying on the spot to enable God to use us as His instruments. If we meet and begin a conversation with a stranger and our conversation curiously lingers, Linda and I silently pray, *Lord, if you are in this, please reveal it to us.* More often than not, the stranger's conversation changes to the subject of faith. A casual chat between strangers suddenly transforms into a divine appointment and results in a blessing for both.

Three years ago, at the trailhead of the New River Rail Trail near Galax in southern Virginia, a woman who had just finished riding approached us. She was just being cordial to some out-of-staters, so we thought. I had just finished my silent prayer when she began sharing about a soup kitchen she started two years earlier. As she went on about how God used her to bless a community she had just moved to with her husband, Linda, my wife, wrote a check for the ministry and handed it to her. The woman introduced herself as Becky, was very grateful, but said she had no intentions of asking us for a donation. "That's okay, Becky," I responded, "perhaps God did?" We parted and began our ride. Two months later, we decided to ride the same trail again and also decided to visit and help out at the kitchen. Later, after cleaning up, Becky told us that the church that had been scheduled to provide the next day's meal had to cancel.

My wife told Becky, "We're on God's time," and then called a local motel and booked a room. The next day, we prepared and served over two hundred grilled cheese sandwiches and salads. This all transpired because we met a stranger in a bike trail parking lot. Months earlier, we intended to bike a new Rail Trail in Virginia. God intended us to help some less fortunate folks—twice. First, we gave a donation and later we devoted our time.

## *Fruit of the Spirit*

Divine appointments, interventions, grace, and the brief reminders we've shared are a fact of the authors' experiences. Because of their frequency, we've begun to wonder whether it has become our calling. It certainly is a ministry to others. The obvious question is "Why?" I believe it is not for us to always know exactly what God plans for our lives. That said, He is, above all else, a God of love. Could it be that the experiences in *A Call to Inspire* were meant to show love in a supernatural way? Could it be nothing more than experiencing the fruit of the Spirit, God's way? *"But the fruit of the Spirit is love, joy, peace, patience, kindness, goodness, faithfulness, gentleness, self-control"* (Galatians 5:22–23, ESV).

## *Opportunity*

What happens when we fail to allow God to use us His way? The answer, I believe, is that we miss an opportunity to please God. We're missing an opportunity to follow Jesus and experience the life He intended for us. If our entire purpose on earth as a believer is to glorify God, then why do we stay in our safe comfort zone? Spiritual growth is about constant change. Since God loves us unconditionally, He wants us to thrive, not just strive and survive.

Glorifying God is not about what we do,
it's about who's doing the work.
—Dr. Lewis W. Gregory, *Introducing the*
*New You.* (Source Ministries 2005)

The Rev. Charles Stanley said this in one of his In Touch daily devotions: "Each Monday morning, I begin the day excited about next Sunday's sermon because I get to share what God is going to teach me that week. Now you may not be a pastor, but you have the same privilege of sharing what the Lord has been teaching you." Linda and I are not trained or ordained pastors, but we are excited about sharing what the Lord has taught us about the Holy Spirit in *A Call to Inspire* and as often as we can.

## Maturity

Are you—we—having difficulty in reaching that level of Christian maturity? Andrew Murray, in *Experiencing the Holy Spirit* (Whittaker House 1984), suggests that insufficient preaching and teaching in our churches and Sunday schools on the Holy Spirit today is the reason why we see so little demonstration of the Spirit in our lives. For the Holy Spirit to use us, Murray suggests, we must surrender our will to God's by exercising faith and trust. Just as in the Acts of the Apostles, it is the work of the Holy Spirit that continues the ministry of Jesus in our lives.

Based on the experiences we shared in *A Call to Inspire*, the authors would certainly concur with Murray's suggestion. The Apostle Paul says in Romans 8:14, that "being led by the Spirit" is how we can live as God's children.

## What Will You Do?

We never know how our words may impact others. If you are a believer, our hope is that you will desire a closer relationship with God that will convict you to be led by the Holy Spirit in your own unique way. The Bible is the greatest story ever told. Proverbs 29:11 tells us that God has a unique plan for our lives, a plan for us to prosper. Yet we know there is a large gap between the glory of that promise and the reality of our experience. The more we draw closer to God, the more closely we draw to His promise. Our hope and prayer is that *A Call to Inspire* just may help you live the story God intended for you. In doing so, perhaps you can bridge that wide chasm between God's will for your life and your desire to see it happen. The decision is yours.

# Epilogue

Linda and I questioned our worth repeatedly in prayer whether to author *A Call to Inspire*. The experiences were totally bizarre to us and supernatural in origin, making it hard to totally comprehend their purpose and meaning other than a rich blessing. Why and how questions were constantly in our thoughts. We consulted pastors and their books.

During our initial experiences, tears would roll down our cheeks each night as we praised and thanked God for using us, just two ordinary folks to do extraordinary things. We may have sincerely prayed for God to use us as His instruments, but we never expected such unimaginable, powerful, and impacting results with complete strangers.

Yet our hearts were filled then and now with pure joy, unimaginable and seemingly limitless joy. It was a joy that refused to be imprisoned and an answered prayer that led to the conviction to write a book. For two years I asked God in prayer for a book title, if He wanted us to author a book. One Sunday, we were led to worship in a downtown Atlanta church, one we never planned to attend that morning. The pastor's message dealt with the Apostle Paul's second letter to the Corinthians. Though the Bible didn't mention the word, the pastor chose the word "inspire" to emphasize Paul's encouragement to the church to be more generous. I looked at Linda and said, "That's it, *A Call to Inspire*."

Yet, as unworthy as we may feel, we must remember that, because of God's unconditional love for us, we are worthy of one thing at least, according to His will—the fruit of the Holy Spirit—

"love, joy, peace, patience, kindness, goodness, faithfulness, gentleness and self-control" (Galatians 5:22–23, ESV).

If you are now reading this, know that it is according to God's will, not that of the authors'. He orchestrated the events. We are just His instruments He used to share them.

There is no greater joy in life than to sense the Holy Spirit at work, for we are all instruments in His orchestra of divine harmony.

—Ken Parkany

# Appendix

An evangelist is one who "has been called and especially equipped by God to declare the Good News to those who have not yet accepted it, with the goal of challenging them to turn to Christ in repentance and faith and to follow Him in obedience to His will."
—Billy Graham, January 1997, in the Preface to his Autobiography, Just as I am (Harper Collins 1997)

# References

Ashurst, Ed. 2013. *Miracle or Coincidence: True Stories about People Living on the Edge.* Nebraska: Morris.

Blackaby, Henry T. and Claude V King. 1994. *Experiencing God.* Tennessee: Broadman & Holman.

Blackaby, Henry and Melvin Blackaby. 2009. *Experiencing the Spirit: The Power of Pentecost Every Day.* Colorado: Multnomah.

Bright, Bill. 1980. *The Holy Spirit: The Key to Supernatural Living.* CA: Campus Crusade for Christ, New Life.

Cho, Paul Yonggi. 1989. *The Holy Spirit, My Senior Partner: Understanding the Holy Spirit & His Gifts.* FL: Creation House.

Goll, James W. 2008. *The Beginner's Guide to Hearing God Speak.* California: Regal.

Graham, Billy. 1997. *Just As I Am: The Autobiography of Billy Graham.* California: Harper Collins.

Gregory, Dr. Lewis W. *The New You: The Ultimate Makeover.* Georgia: Source Ministries

Harris, Randall (Compiled). 2004. *The Contemporaries Meet the Classics on The Holy Spirit.* Los Angeles: Howard.

Horton, Stanley M. 1997. *What the Bible Says About the Holy Spirit.* Missouri: Gospel Publishing House, 8th Printing.

Hillman, Os. 2002. *How to Know and Do the Will of God.* Georgia: Asian Group Publishing.

Idleman, Kyle. 2011. *Not a Fan.* Michigan: Zondervan.

Jacks, Bob and Matthew R. Jacks with Pam Mellskog. 2002. *Divine Appointments.* Colorado: Navpress.

Johnson, Bill. 2003. *When Heaven Invades Earth, A Practical Guide to a Life of Miracles.* Pennsylvania: Destiny House Publishers.

Lawrence, Brother. 1982. *The Practice of the Presence of God.* Pennsylvania: Whittaker House.

Lucado, Max. 1999. *When God Whispers Your Name.* Tennessee: Word Publishing.

Matthews, John. 2009. *The Divine Purpose: Displayed in the Works of Providence and Grace.* Alabama: Solid Ground Christian Books.

McQuilkin, Robertson. 2000. *Life in the Spirit.* Tennessee: Broadman & Holman

Murray, Andrew. 1984. *Experiencing The Holy Spirit* (Formerly titled *In Search of Spiritual Excellence*). Pennsylvania: Whittaker House.

Olsen, Roger D. 2004. *Keeping Divine Appointments: It Can Be as Natural as Breathing!* Tennessee: Amazing Grace Mission.

Packer, J.I. 1973. *Knowing God.* Illinois: Intervarsity Press. 1984. *Keep in Step with The Spirit.* New Jersey: Fleming H. Revell.

Peale, Norman Vincent. 1967. *Enthusiasm Makes the Difference.* New York: Guideposts. 1994. *Words That Inspired Him.* New York: Inspirational Press.

Prater, Arnold. 1993 *The Presence: The Ministry of the Holy Spirit.* Tennessee: Thomas Nelson.

Rushnell, Squire. 2006. *When God Winks at You.* Tennessee: Thomas Nelson. 2001. *When God Winks.* New York: Atria Books.

Stanley, Charles. 1996. *Listening to God: In Touch Study Series.* Tennessee: Thomas Nelson. 1996. *Relying on The Holy Spirit: In Touch Series.* Tennessee: Thomas Nelson.

Swindoll, Charles R. 1993. *Flying Closer to the Flame: A Passion for The Holy Spirit.* Texas: Word Publishing.

# About the Author

Ken and Linda Parkany served as lay pastors in their Connecticut church for over thirty years. They both are trained Stephen Ministers in a nondenominational care-giving ministry to those in crisis. Ken is a retired aerospace and aviation business professional, having spent thirty-seven years with United Technologies Corporation—Pratt & Whitney Division. Ken is also a former freelance outdoor writer, and weekly columnist with the Hartford Courant in Connecticut. As a lifelong fly fisherman, he compiled and edited *The Flyfishers Companion*, privately published in 1992 by the Connecticut Fly Fishermen's Association. Linda is a retired registered nurse, a lifelong caregiver, a devoted mother and grandmother affectionately called Beeba. Together they are passionate Rails-to-Trails cyclists, byway travelers and divine appointment seekers. Parents to three married children and twelve grandchildren, they currently reside in Cumming, Georgia. Since 2011, they've posted many of their amazing travel experiences and photos at: www.happytrails2u.weebly.com.

CPSIA information can be obtained
at www.ICGtesting.com
Printed in the USA
LVHW012208080519
617179LV00003B/5/P